"Incredibly quick-witted while challenging. It meets you right where you are and immediately inspires you to grow from there. Susanna's humor and realness connect you with her in such a way that you feel like you've made a true friend. I believe that's a gift, and she most certainly has it."

—**Tiffany Arbuckle Lee**, aka Plumb,
songwriter and Curb Records recording artist

"With beautiful writing, humor, and depth of insight, Susanna Foth Aughtmon unpacks one of the most important stories in the Bible and reveals truth every woman needs to hear. No more listening to lying snakes for me!"

—**Joanna Weaver**, bestselling author,
Having a Mary Heart in a Martha World

Also by Susanna Foth Aughtmon

All I Need Is Jesus and a Good Pair of Jeans: The Tired Supergirl's Search for Grace

My Bangs Look Good and Other Lies I Tell Myself: The Tired Supergirl's Search for Truth

I Blame EVE

Freedom from Perfectionism, Control Issues, and the Tendency to Listen to Talking Snakes

SUSANNA FOTH AUGHTMON

a division of Baker Publishing Group
Grand Rapids, Michigan

Published by Revell
a division of Baker Publishing Group
P.O. Box 6287, Grand Rapids, MI 49516-6287
www.revellbooks.com

Printed in the United States of America

Library of Congress Cataloging-in-Publication Data
Aughtmon, Susanna Foth, 1970–
I blame Eve : freedom from perfectionism, control issues, and the tendency to listen to talking snakes / Susanna Foth Aughtmon.
p. cm.
ISBN 978-0-8007-2047-6 (pbk.)
1. Temptation. 2. Sin. 3. Eve (Biblical figure) 4. Christian life. I. Title.
BT725.A844 2012
248.8′43—dc23 2011046571

Published in association with the literary agency Books & Such, 52 Mission Circle #122 PMB 170, Santa Rosa, California 95409.

12 13 14 15 16 17 18 7 6 5 4 3 2 1

For Dick and Ruth Foth,
whose good, strong love helped me grow
up and gave me wings to fly.
Dad and Mom,
your love for Jesus and each other
has shaped me irrevocably.
I want to grow up to be like you.
I love you the most.

Contents

Acknowledgments

G. B. Stern said, "Silent gratitude isn't much use to anyone." And that is the truth. I have so many people to be thankful for, and I am choosing not to be silent about it. So a huge amount of thanks goes out to . . .

Scott. You are my favorite person. Thank you for loving me so well and always encouraging me, for taking care of the boys so well and always making me laugh . . . even when I have a deadline.

Jack, Will, and Addison. Thanks for all your hugs and kisses, even though I was writing *so* much. I love who you are. It is my great joy to be your mom.

Mom and Dad. Thanks for lighting a candle and praying for me as I wrote. And for eating celebratory chocolate chips with me when I finally finished. You are the best.

Dave and Lola. Thanks for your constant support and for cheering me on every time I call you. (Yeah, Sue!) You are the best in-laws ever. (Yeah, Dave! Yeah, Lola!)

Erica and Jenny. Thanks for listening to my chapters over the phone and laughing at all the right parts. And for celebrating the fun stuff with me. Whether it is a birthday or another chapter finished or a shopping trip, you make everything fun. I love being with you.

Chris. I'm proud to be your sister. Writing about catching snakes with you at the house on Glen Canyon brought back good memories. About you . . . not the snakes.

The Foth, Moody, Clements, and Bondonno clans. I am so thankful for you and your encouragement. I'm so glad you are my family. Clearly, I lucked out!

My teenage nieces and nephew, Aly, Claire, Robert, and Katherine. Know that it was for you that I wrote "holla" in this book, mostly because I wanted to see your look of horror at your aunt pretending to be hip. Know that I think you are beyond hip and I love you.

Beth Alyse Alyse and Gretchen. Our day in Burlingame was a highlight for me. I could not ask for better cousins. Thank you for your constant love and encouragement.

Jenn. Thanks for being my bff and partner in crime. Does teaching count as crime? I'm so thankful for you. Someday soon we'll do the running man again. I promise.

Marty. Thanks for always being real and sharing your chocolate and letting me tell some of your story. I'm so thankful for your friendship.

Paula. Thank you, dear friend, for your friendship, for the many meals made for our family, and for subbing for me so I could write. You will get an extra jewel in your crown for sure.

Pathway Church. Thanks for being a part of this writing journey. I will try to be a less awkward worship leader in the future. But thanks for loving me as I am.

Tapestry Church and Kiddie Garden Preschool. You are a blessing to me. I'm so thankful for you.

Janelle Mahlmann. Thanks for your hard work and for always laughing with me on the phone. I love working with you.

Vicki Crumpton. To get to work with you again is such fun. I am thankful to you for your giftedness and excitement about this book. I love that I get to share this writing journey with you.

Wendy Lawton. I think you are the best in the land. I love that we are on the same team. I am continually thankful that God brought you into my life.

I would be remiss not to thank Eve. Without her there would be no book.

And finally, thanks goes to Jesus, for letting me write, of course, but most of all for saving me from my controlling, perfectionist ways and shaping my life with his grace and freedom.

Adam and Eve's Story

This is the account of the creation of the heavens and the earth.

When the LORD God made the heavens and the earth, there were no plants or grain growing on the earth, for the LORD God had not sent any rain. And no one was there to cultivate the soil. But water came up out of the ground and watered all the land. And the LORD God formed a man's body from the dust of the ground and breathed into it the breath of life. And the man became a living person.

Then the LORD God planted a garden in Eden, in the east, and there he placed the man he had created. And the LORD God planted all sorts of trees in the garden—beautiful trees that produced delicious fruit. At the center of the garden he placed the tree of life and the tree of the knowledge of good and evil.

A river flowed from the land of Eden, watering the garden and then dividing into four branches. One of these branches is the Pishon, which flows around the entire land of Havilah, where gold is found. The gold of that land is exceptionally pure; aromatic resin and onyx stone are also found there. The second branch is the Gihon, which flows around the entire land of Cush. The third branch is the Tigris, which flows to the east of Asshur. The fourth branch is the Euphrates.

The LORD God placed the man in the Garden of Eden to tend and care for it. But the LORD God gave him this warning: "You may freely eat any fruit in the garden except fruit from the tree of the knowledge of good and evil. If you eat of its fruit, you will surely die."

And the LORD God said, "It is not good for the man to be alone. I will make a companion who will help him." So the LORD God formed from the soil every kind of animal and bird. He brought them to Adam to see what he would call them, and Adam chose a name for each one. He gave names to all the livestock, birds, and wild animals. But still there was no companion suitable for him. So the LORD God caused Adam to fall into a deep sleep. He took one of Adam's ribs and closed up the place from which he had taken it. Then the LORD God made a woman from the rib and brought her to Adam.

"At last!" Adam exclaimed. "She is part of my own flesh and bone! She will be called 'woman,' because she was taken out of a man." This explains why a man leaves his father and mother and is joined to his wife, and the two are united into one. Now, although Adam and his wife were both naked, neither of them felt any shame.

Now the serpent was the shrewdest of all the creatures the LORD God had made. "Really?" he asked the woman. "Did God really say that you must not eat any of the fruit in the garden?"

"Of course we may eat it," the woman told him. "It's only the fruit from the tree at the center of the garden that we are not allowed to eat. God says we must not eat it or even touch it, or we will die."

"You won't die!" the serpent hissed. "God knows that your eyes will be opened when you eat it. You will become just like God, knowing everything, both good and evil."

The woman was convinced. The fruit looked so fresh and delicious, and it would make her so wise! So she ate some of the fruit. She also gave some to her husband, who was with her. Then he ate it, too. At that moment, their eyes were opened, and they suddenly felt shame at their nakedness. So they strung fig leaves together around their hips to cover themselves.

Toward evening they heard the LORD God walking about in the garden, so they hid themselves among the trees. The LORD God called to Adam, "Where are you?"

He replied, "I heard you, so I hid. I was afraid because I was naked."

"Who told you that you were naked?" the LORD God asked. "Have you eaten the fruit I commanded you not to eat?"

"Yes," Adam admitted, "but it was the woman you gave me who brought me the fruit, and I ate it."

Then the LORD God asked the women, "How could you do such a thing?"

"The serpent tricked me," she replied. "That's why I ate it."

So the LORD God said to the serpent, "Because you have done this, you will be punished. You are singled out from all the domestic and wild animals of the whole earth to be cursed. You will grovel in the dust as long as you live, crawling along on your belly. From now on, you and the woman will be enemies, and your offspring and her offspring will be enemies. He will crush your head, and you will strike his heel."

Then he said to the woman, "You will bear children with intense pain and suffering. And though your desire will be for your husband, he will be your master."

And to Adam he said, "Because you listened to your wife and ate the fruit I told you not to eat, I have placed a curse on the ground. All your life you will struggle to scratch a living from it. It will grow thorns and thistles for you, though you will eat of its grains. All your life you will sweat to produce food, until your dying day. Then you will return to the ground from which you came. For you were made from dust, and to the dust you will return."

Then Adam named his wife Eve, because she would be the mother of all people everywhere. And the LORD God made clothing from animal skins for Adam and his wife.

Then the LORD God said, "The people have become as we are, knowing everything, both good and evil. What if they eat the fruit of the tree of life? Then they will live forever!" So the LORD God banished Adam and his wife from the Garden of Eden, and he sent Adam out to cultivate the ground from which he had been made. After banishing them from the garden, the LORD God stationed mighty angelic beings to the east of Eden. And a flaming sword flashed back and forth, guarding the way to the tree of life.

Genesis 2:4–3:24

Introduction

I Want a Perfect Life

In the beginning God created the heavens and the earth. Then Eve came along and messed it up. Of course, she had a little help from that no-good snake, and, just for the record, Adam didn't do a whole lot to dissuade a sister from taking down all of humanity with her poor judgment. One day life for all humankind is perfect, and the next day everything goes terribly wrong.

Every once in a while I have a deep thought. Mostly I think about decorating magazines and chocolate, but one morning I was thinking about Eve and her choice to eat the apple. I thought to myself, *She had it all—a loving husband, an unhindered relationship with God, all of her needs taken care of. She could walk around naked and not feel like crying inside. Her life was perfect . . . and she still wasn't satisfied.*

It was an epiphany for me. She was perfect. Her life was perfect. And she thought she could do better. How did she think she could outdo perfect? She was everything she was meant to be. She was living the dream. She had the perfect life. And she blew it. I would have liked a shot at that pre-apple, perfect life.

A life without trial. A day without heartache. A thigh without ripples. It's hard to imagine a life like that, but I try. I think about what it would be like not to sin. I ponder what it would feel like to be gracious and humble without feeling like my spleen might burst. (Maybe you have never felt your spleen before, but often, when you must do something against your nature, there can be a distinct tightening in the gut. That is your spleen.) I delight in thinking about not having to suck in my stomach. I had three overly large babies in five years. The stomach situation is not pretty. At this point, my brain starts hurting, trying to wrap itself around the thought of me being perfect because it is so far out of the realm of possibility . . . because of Eve. I blame Eve.

My nine-year-old son, Jack, and I were sitting on the couch discussing life the other afternoon. We were discussing deep things like video games and swimming lessons when a genuine philosophical question popped up. He wanted to know if babies go to heaven when they die.

And I said, "Yes."

And then he said, "What about three-year-olds?"

And I said, "Yes."

And then he paused and said, "What about nine-year-olds? Do they go to heaven when they die . . . even if they don't know Jesus?"

(This was the important question. Obviously, his fate hung in the balance here.)

I paused while trying to retrieve some knowledge I'd acquired in my systematic theology class in college.

"I think only God gets to decide that, Jack. He knows when each nine-year-old becomes aware of their sinfulness and when they are old enough to understand about him."

"Well, I'm aware of my sinfulness," he said. He punched his fist into his palm. "Man, Mom! If God hadn't taken out Adam's rib, everything would be perfect!"

Even my son blames Eve. This belief often comes to light at the tender age when we realize, "Sweet hosannas, I've got problems, and I think it's someone else's fault that I'm so messed up!"

Maybe you don't blame Eve. Maybe you offer your life, imperfections and all, to the glory of God. Maybe you don't struggle with perfectionism or have control issues. Maybe you don't hyperventilate when you feel like your world is spinning out of control. Maybe you think cellulite is cute. Maybe you take responsibility for all your poor choices and your sin nature. Good for you. You are obviously much more spiritual than I am.

I would like to imagine that all my life's unhappiness and my general inability to be holy are Eve's fault. Because she couldn't say no to herself and she didn't think God had her best interests at heart. Because the lies of the snake sounded better than God's truth. Because fruit, especially forbidden fruit, is so tasty. She messed up. So now I mess up, and I blame her.

My husband, Scott, says that I better be careful when I get to heaven because Eve is not going to appreciate my slanderous words in this book. She might not like me pointing out her shortcomings. Scott thinks she might be on the lookout for me when I arrive at the pearly gates and konk me in the head with a symbolic apple. She might. Or she might just want to have a heartfelt chat with me about how, if she could, she would take that bite back. She might say, "I missed the point completely. It wasn't about God keeping good things from me. I get that now." Or she might say, "I am really so sorry about the whole childbirth thing. Who could have seen that coming?" Then we will sit down with a cup of coffee (of course there is coffee in heaven!) and while away a good portion of eternity talking about life and mistakes and why we are so thankful that God loves us just as we are . . . even though not one of us is perfect. And then after Eve and I have declared ourselves bfih (best friends in heaven), I will have to whisper a terrible truth in Eve's ear—the truth that if she hadn't eaten the apple and by some miracle no one else had eaten the apple until my lifetime, I would have done it. No doubt about it. And on the off chance that I couldn't get to the tree, it probably would've been you grabbing for the fruit.

Maybe that is why you picked up this book. You, like Eve and me, want more than God is offering you. You're not content with life as you know it. You too yearn for a perfect life, or maybe you want a smidge of control. Maybe you have found that neatly ordering your life doesn't set you free like you thought it would. Or you have struggled with trying to run your world and have found out, to your great surprise, that you are no good at it. Maybe you have known Jesus for nearly all your life and are just now realizing that you need him every day and even more on Sundays. (Why are Sundays so difficult?) Maybe you are just tired. And you would like a bit of peace. I'm right there with you.

So here we are longing for some freedom from our mess and a bit of Eden in our crazy lives. We are hoping to learn something from Eve and her mistakes. From her desire to design her own destiny. From her choice to walk out on the One who loved her best. The One who loves us best. And the best part is that the God of the universe who created you is tickled to death that you are on this journey of loving him back and searching for answers, even when you are not quite sure what it is you are looking for half the time. He, more than anything, would like to set you free . . . from the cage of perfectionism, from the hold of control issues, from the lies of the snake, from the feelings of hopelessness that pin you down when you feel your world spinning out of control, and from the unholy anger that grips you when your plans go awry. Doesn't that sound fantastic? It is, actually. So without further hesitation, let's get on with it. Because it's about to get good.

1

I Wish Eve Hadn't Eaten the Apple

Just for the record, you probably noticed that in Genesis there is no mention of an apple. It says that Eve ate the fruit. So really it could have been a nice plum or a juicy peach that Eve nibbled on, for all we know. But if I were to ask you to close your eyes and imagine Eve in all her glory, reaching for that piece of forbidden fruit, very few of you would picture Eve grabbing a lovely kumquat. When we think Eve, we think apple. And most of us are going with a Red Delicious apple in our mind's eye. So for the sake of our own apple bias, I will refer to the unnamed fruit of the tree of the knowledge of good and evil as an apple. But I will not stop you from being creative in your own thinking as you read. When I say "apple," feel free to think persimmon if you are so inclined.

Now that we are all clear on that, you may wonder why I wish Eve hadn't eaten the apple. Here are forty reasons in no particular order of importance:

1. female facial hair (mustaches, unibrows, etc.—I'm positive these are evidence of the fall)
2. garbage
3. miscommunication
4. exercise videos
5. corns (on your feet, not on the cob)
6. cancer
7. violence
8. warts
9. bad fiction
10. smog
11. man-eating sharks
12. human trafficking
13. body shapers (i.e., girdles—let's just call them what they are)
14. depression
15. grass stains
16. death
17. cold showers
18. potty talk
19. stinging nettles
20. shots (I know they are good for you, but I hate the poking part)
21. hurt feelings
22. broken friendships
23. cockroaches
24. cicadas
25. fire ants (I could continue to list insects, but I will refrain for the sake of the list's integrity)
26. racial tension
27. body odor
28. genocide
29. bullies
30. texting lingo (I don't really think this is Eve's fault, but it is annoying, and if life were perfect, I wouldn't be annoyed, so I am including this in the list . . . lol)
31. weight gain
32. dirty laundry (remember, Adam and Eve didn't wear clothes; ergo, no laundry)
33. traffic violations
34. poverty
35. land mines
36. spider veins
37. long lines
38. money problems
39. bloating
40. arm flab (that wing-like appendage on the back of your arm that continues waving to your friend after you have finished)

From the life shattering to the inane, there are so many reasons to be upset at Eve. Now don't get me wrong. I don't think Eve set out to bring about the destruction of the world when she bit into the apple. I don't think she had that much foresight. But I do think she was completely unaware of how fantastic her existence was. I don't think she was thinking about how carefully God had planned on her and Adam's behalf. He had created a place where he could hang out with his creation, giving them breath and hope and freedom. He provided for them body, mind, and spirit. God intended for them to have a glorious and blessed life, a perfect life in his presence.

And Eve was clueless. She had no idea what perfect was, even though she embodied it. She was exactly the person God intended her to be. She had no faults inside or out. She looked exactly the way she was supposed to look. That in and of itself is no small thing. When I think about how comfortable she must have been in her own skin, I tend to get irritable. She never once had to say to Adam, "Do I look fat? Oh, wait, never mind. I forgot I'm perfect." Or even better, she had no preconceived ideas of what beauty is. Eve was all that a woman was meant to be, and she owned it.

She had a perfect relationship with Adam—they completed each other, for heaven's sake. There were no miscommunications. No misinterpreted feelings. No I-have-no-idea-what-you-are-trying-to-tell-me-can-we-get-someone-over-here-who-speaks-man-lingo moments.

I think about what it would be like to understand my husband, Scott, completely, and vice versa. That type of communication would revolutionize our marriage. I would know that when Scott says he had a good day that it means he actually had a good day . . . no hidden meanings or layers of unread emotion. And in return, when I say I had a good day, Scott would know that I still need to engage in a forty-five-minute discourse on how my friends and I are getting along so well and the boys are growing up beautifully and even though I am struggling to control my chocolate addiction I ate only half a bar of chocolate today instead of a whole bar and so it was, you know, a good day.

Even better, Eve had no weird ideas about God. There were no theological quandaries. No "I wonder if God is real" questions. Of course he was real. She could see him standing under that flowering plum tree with Adam. And as for feeling his presence in her life on a regular basis? She could meet up with him and have a nice heart-to-heart talk. Can you imagine having a one-on-one conversation with the living God? The God who hangs stars and forms planets with his words? That God? That is simply beyond my comprehension.

As for daily living, there were no stressors in her life. The world acted like it was supposed to act. Every single aspect of her life was flawless, running like clockwork. God had breathed life into her and had set her in the midst of a beautiful life fashioned after his design. There was no loneliness, bitterness, hardship, anger, coveting, lying, or wrinkles. And after they had put in a hard day's work, which would have been fun in their perfect garden, Adam and Eve got to sit around naked and unashamed. Naked and unashamed. Now that is an oxymoron if I have ever heard one. In my world, if you are sitting around naked, there is shame aplenty. And if you don't have the good sense to be ashamed of your naked self, I'll do it for you. We live worlds apart, pre-apple Eve and I.

I know in my heart that Eve did not realize the chain of events she would set in motion with that bite. How could she know that thousands of years later people would still be dealing with her mess? She couldn't know the horror of cancer. No one had ever gotten sick before. She couldn't know about stinging nettles. All the plants in the garden were sting-free. And what about fear? Anxiety? Depression? She couldn't have had a clue. Her life was held in God's palm. She didn't know what would happen once she stepped out of his palm into a world of her own making.

I keep wondering if there wasn't more to the conversation God had with Adam and Eve about what would happen if they decided to eat from the tree of knowledge. Did he give them the whole rundown of everything that would go awry if they ate the forbidden fruit? Did he tell them the life they knew would completely break down and the consequences of their actions would resonate until the end of time? Did they know that from that moment on they would be broken versions of the people he had created them to be? I don't know. But he did tell them the end result of their action. Death. Did they know what death would look like? That it would be the loss of hope and freedom and joy? That days would be filled with hard work and a side of crankiness? That death could mean a thousand kinds of dying each day?

They must have understood that death would be a permanent, horrible thing. But apparently, something deep within Eve still made her want to do what she knew she shouldn't. An unction propelled her to go forward no matter what the consequences were. There must have been some feeling lurking about in her soul that said, "I know God is in charge, but I'm still going to do what I want to do anyway." Sound familiar?

I get the same response from my five-year-old son, Addison.

My mom and dad recently brought me an old blanket chest to use as a coffee table. We painted it a lovely bright white, and Addison wanted to help paint the legs. Before I handed him the brush, I looked at him and said, "This paint is wet. Don't touch it with your finger." So he immediately touched it with his finger. Immediately. I wanted to say, "Have you recently experienced hearing loss that I am unaware of?" Instead, I said, "Addison! Why did you just do what I told you not to do?" His answer was brilliant. A shrug of the shoulders and an "I don't know."

I am pretty sure this was Eve's response when she was asked, "Why? Why did you do it?" A shoulder shrug. A confused pondering of, "Now why did I think that eating that apple would be so great?" Eve just knew that she wanted more than God was offering, more than she was allowed to take. And her critical-thinking skills stalled out there.

Poor Eve. And poor us. The ones who do exactly as she did. We have so little ability to imagine the consequences of our actions. We act without thinking about where an action will take us. We step out of God's palm into a world of our own making with our own sad choices and shoddy reasoning. We experience death in a thousand ways each day as we flounder around looking for that place where everything comes together exactly as we think it should. We are still looking for Eden. For perfection and rightness and unbridled joy. The more we try to get there using our crafty manipulations, the farther away we move from God's hand. His plans. His goodness. His world. We wonder how we can be so far from the place we are supposed to be and the person we are meant to be. We wonder how we can feel so hopeless and so desperate when we are giving it our all in this life we've been given.

Well, it begins the same way for us as it began for our sister Eve. It begins with the voice of doubt and chaos, the voice that invites us to wonder if we don't deserve more than we've been given. It begins with the thought that no one can tell us what to do. It begins with a hiss and a mirthless laugh as we wander far away from the heart of the One who breathed life into us. It begins with the snake.

2

I Would Listen to a Talking Snake

There is something alluring about a creature who can talk. When a critter who is not normally supposed to talk opens its mouth and speaks, it is a phenomenon. It's magical. A crowd pleaser. I know this because I witness it on a regular basis. Every week we go to the shopping center down the street from our house. We are going for groceries, but inevitably the boys have to take a detour to the restaurant next to the grocery store because of the talking parrot. Every day his cage sits on the sidewalk, and he welcomes the patrons with his chatter. There is usually a small cluster of children or an adult or two near the cage as the parrot preens and squawks and says, "Hello!" numerous times. The kids don't tire of it. They all mimic the bird and answer back, saying, "Hello." The bird wields a certain power over his audience. As long as he is talking, people are engaged. As soon as he stops talking, he is just another bird on a wire, and the crowd walks away.

[illegible] one can make while chatting with our neigh- [illegible] rrot is that because he is saying, “Hello!” one [illegible] think this parrot is actually friendly. And then one [illegible] thinking that maybe the parrot wants to be friends and [illegible] ould like to shake hands or something. This could not be further from the truth. I know this because on the parrot’s cage is a rather large sign that says, “Do not put your fingers in the cage. The bird bites,” or something of that nature. This always makes me think, *Who first discovered that the bird bites?* I feel sad for that person. And I am hyperattentive to my children’s fingers because I have a fondness for their fingers and don’t want them to lose them. Each time we go near the bird, I remind my kids, “Don’t touch the bird. Just because the bird is chatting you up doesn’t mean he likes you.” But it seems like an easy mistake to make. Just ask Eve.

Eve knows all about being at the mercy of a talking critter. I don’t know how Eve felt when the snake sidled up next to her. But she didn’t seem scared or wary, which she really should have been. His charming words seemed to catch her off guard. What Eve didn’t know or seem to suspect was that the snake was shrewd and had a plan in targeting her. He was a talking creature with a vendetta. This did not bode well for Eve. He was out for payback against the Creator. The snake was a low-down-rotten-no-good-try-to-hurt-God-any-way-he-could kind of creature. (There is a reason that snakes give us the willies other than the fact that they have weird tongues. The first of their kind led to our demise.) With his silky voice, he had Eve at word one. Just like the talking parrot mesmerizes his sidewalk audience, the talking snake charmed Eve. He had her attention. All of it. And she had no idea that this snake’s bite was deadly.

This snake had a way with words. Listen to what he said. "Really? Did God really say you must not eat any of the fruit in the garden?" This sounded like genuine concern on the snake's part, like he didn't want her missing out on anything. The truth was that the snake actually had no concern for Eve at all and was twisting what God had said so that it sounded right in Eve's ears. He wasn't fond of God . . . still isn't; hates him actually. So messing with God's creation was fun for him. Really fun. The snake wanted Eve on the defensive and off guard so he could get her doubting. Wondering. It was a brilliant ploy, actually. He just had to introduce some confusion and mistrust and let Eve's brain do the rest.

I want to yell out to Eve, "Stick your fingers in your ears! Don't listen to him. He's no good!" Obviously, my yelling is a few millennia too late, because the lying had begun and Eve was falling for it. The snake didn't just want to bite her finger, parrot style. The snake was bent on destroying Eve. Completely. He wasn't asking Eve a question. He was calling God into question. The snake was saying, in essence, "I think God is lying to you, don't you?"

Eve made a critical mistake. The problem was not that this creature was messing with her or that what he was saying was ridiculous. The problem was that Eve didn't turn on her heel and walk away. Eve paused a moment and gave his words credence. She weighed them against her own logic and what she recalled God saying to her. She did what so many of us have done on way too many occasions. Eve listened to the enemy of her soul.

I find it interesting that Eve didn't check in with God to see if the snake was on the up and up. She knew God. She had a relationship with the One who had formed her from dust and Adam's bone. At any moment, she could have decided to tell this sneaky creature, "What you are saying has me completely captivated, but I'm just going to check in with the guy who made me to see if what you are saying is true." But instead of touching base with God, Eve began to consider the possibility that maybe God wasn't being entirely up-front about things. She began to doubt him. And this was the beginning of the end.

Eve was not unlike us in our everyday living when we lose sight of the One who made us and begin to have doubts. We may not acknowledge that we are perplexed or wavering in our faith, but somehow these doubts weave their way into our thoughts and camp out in our souls. Does God really love me? Does he really have good plans for me? What did he really say about that area of my life that I struggle with so often? I can't seem to recall his words. But this talking snake really sounds like he knows what he is talking about. Before we know it, we too can be charmed by the snake and his twisted truths. All too quickly, we forget the words of the Creator and start listening to the words of the snake. We become unmoored from the firm truth of the One who made us. We are cast adrift in a sea of doubt and confusion, and all of a sudden we are doubting our Maker right along with Eve.

There is only one thing to be done about these doubts. Do the thing that Eve forgot to do. Run. Run back to the One who formed you with his hands. Run as fast as your little legs can carry you and start calling out to him, "God? Are you there? It's me. I'm full of doubts and awash in untruths that the stupid snake told me! I need you to tell me again what you said. Remind me how you saved me with your grace. Right now I am completely confused, and that snake is sounding better by the minute!" Or, "Jesus, talking snakes are such attention getters. I have a hard time not listening to their chatter. Please speak loudly and remind me that you came to set me free from the lies of my enemy. Tell me that you have more for me than the snake ever could. I need you."

It is important to invite God into the snaky conversations that take place in our minds and the niggling doubts that dig into our souls, because this is where the battle begins, sister. The battle of good versus evil. The war of right versus wrong. And, of course, snake versus God. Our battle begins in our hearts and minds when we are feeling alone and wavering in our knowledge of what is right and true. The fight begins when we choose to run toward the truth even when the untruth seems so much better. It begins when we decide we are not willing to take the snake at his word. It begins when we turn our back on the snake, no matter how slick talking he is, and start calling out to God, the author and finisher of our faith, to set us straight with his words. His power. His rightness. His grace.

The best part about calling out to God is that he hears us. He does. And he is excited to know that we want to hear what he has to say, because he loves telling us the truth. Because he is the Truth, and we need to recognize him for who he is. We begin making our way back toward God when we seek his truth. In this journey of owning up to our stuff and seeking to know the One who created us, let's invite the truth to be a part of this process. A prayer together would be a good way to start. Let's do it together, shall we?

God,
I have done a whole lot of listening to the snake in my lifetime.

I've listened to my doubts instead of running back to you.
Forgive me for listening to lies.
Show me how to follow you.
Help me to recognize your voice.
Fill me with your presence.
And cover me with your grace.
I love you.
Amen.

3

I Think God Is Holding Out on Me

A wise woman (my sister Erica) once said to me, "Don't ever take your children to Toys R Us. Ever." Now you may think that is a harsh statement. That's what I thought, anyway. What I failed to recognize was that Erica was speaking from rich experience. She had years of child rearing under her belt. Erica wasn't trying to hold me back. She was trying to prevent me from experiencing the beast that lurks within the breasts of all innocent children, the one that is unleashed the moment a young child is denied what he or she wants at Toys R Us. She wanted to protect me from the shrieks of a child that can undo the calmest of mothers and make them want to rip their own ears off.

I ignored her wisdom one day and took my sons Jack and Will, then ages four and two, to Toys R Us. We were going to buy a gift for an upcoming birthday party. It was blissfully calm as I browsed and they played with some small wooden trains on a nearby train table. At least it was blissfully calm until I selected the gift and said, "Okay, boys. Let's go." A cry of torment rent the heavens because what they heard was, "Okay, boys, Mommy wants to take away everything you ever wanted in your short, sweet lives."

I will not go into all the gory details, but there was some egregious howling. You have never known the freakish strength of a toddler until you try to loose his tiny grip on a Thomas train. I abandoned all thoughts of purchasing the gift in hopes of making it out of the store with my sanity. Their shrieks pierced the air as we winged our way toward the exit. Clearly, the children saw our departure as some form of child abuse. The well-known threat of parents everywhere, "Just wait until we get home!" issued forth from my lips. I passed other shoppers, their eyebrows raised in disdain at the sheer ear-piercing volume of my offspring. I found myself thinking in military terms, "The mission has been compromised! Abort mission! Go! Go! Go!" I had one objective: to get out of Toys R Us and never come back again.

The boys were clearly unhappy with me. They thought I had the keys to the proverbial toy kingdom and was not sharing them. In their eyes, I was a terrible mother and a selfish woman. To an egocentric toddler and preschooler, the very thought that I would not give them their hearts' desire made me their enemy. Plain and simple.

It seems that my egocentric toddler and preschooler had a lot in common with our sister Eve. All of a sudden Eve wanted something she couldn't have. A big, fat, juicy apple. And to make matters worse, Eve started to listen to the hissing prattle of the snake. "You won't die. God knows that your eyes will be opened when you eat it. You will become just like God, knowing everything, both good and evil."

It's almost as if Eve entered her own personal toy store. "I won't die? My eyes will be opened? I'll know everything? That's all I've ever wanted. One of each, please!" Okay, maybe she had never thought about these things before, but after the snake mentioned them, how could she not want them? And why wouldn't God give her what she wanted? Obviously, he was threatened by her and didn't want her to become like him. He was holding out on her.

Have you ever really wanted something? So much that it hurt? You knew it wouldn't be that great for you in the long run, but, sweet mercy, if you couldn't get your hands on it you might just keel over and throw a toy store tantrum. I had a relationship or three like that in my dating years. I thought if I wasn't in a relationship that I would waste away to nothing. I felt like I was less than a person if a boy didn't like me. This growing want deep within me began to overtake all clear thinking. I wanted what I wanted, and here I was boyfriendless. Clearly, God was holding out on me, so I would just have to take matters into my own hands.

This is never a good place to be. Not for Jack or Will or Eve or me or you, for that matter. The whole taking-matters-into-your-own-hands bit is a bust for all of us. That great chasm of want that wells up within our souls has a name. Desire. For Jack and Will it was every train in Toys R Us. For Eve it was knowledge. For me it was a relationship. For you it might be something else. Desire can scream so loudly in our souls that we cannot hear anything else. There is almost nothing we won't do if we really want something. Our desires give birth to temptation.

Jesus's brother James talked about temptation. He said, "Temptation comes from the lure of our own evil desires.

These evil desires lead to evil actions, and evil actions lead to death. So don't be misled, my dear brothers and sisters" (James 1:14–16).

James nailed it. That is what temptation does. It misleads us. It walks us right onto a path that leads to no good whatsoever. Eve started walking out of the garden long before she ever bit into the apple. She heard the hiss and lure of that snaky voice, and it birthed a desire within her, a desire for control, a desire for knowledge, a desire to take more than God was giving. One step, then two steps, then three steps, and all of a sudden she was on the brink of changing the course of human history.

It all seemed to happen so suddenly. How did Eve suddenly find herself in the middle of Eden underneath that forbidden tree, smacking her lips? How did that apple find its way into her hand, fitting so perfectly into her palm? How did she come to press it to her lips? Just yesterday she was chatting with God and Adam about the beauty of the sunset. How did she end up here today?

The snake is so subtle. That is his evil genius. Sin doesn't start with an action. It starts with a thought. A phrase or an impression flitting across the mind. A twisting of the truth that seems more advantageous to us. The suggestion gets us thinking or wanting or longing for something that God is not offering us. Suddenly, we are baby stepping away from God's purpose for our lives, throwing caution to the wind, wanting what we want, and not giving one thought to what lies in store for us after we get what we want. What we don't realize is that we are walking away from the One who loves us most toward the one who wants to destroy us. We are walking away from life and heading toward death. I'm not trying to be melodramatic. I'm just quoting James. Evil actions lead to death—maybe not an immediate physical death, but surely spiritual and emotional death is soon to follow.

I died a million small deaths trying to fulfill the desire that haunted me, that moved me to make poor decisions and left me reeling when they backfired. Broken friendships. Heartache. Loss. Feeling far from God and misunderstood. I lost the sense of who I was in God's eyes and in my own, for that matter. I was lonely and desperate. I walked away from the One who loved me best. I followed in Eve's footsteps and found disaster in her wake. I thought God wouldn't give me what I wanted. In reality, God wouldn't give me what would destroy me. He loved me too much. I forgot about that. He wasn't holding out on me. He was trying to hold me, close to his heart and his truth. He was trying to save me from myself.

God can't stand for us to be far away from him. It makes him nuts to see us running blindly toward the thing that will hurt us most. He doesn't want to see us broken, crying, hurting because we followed the path of desire and ended up with less than we had to start with. God wants us near. Near enough to hear his truth. Near enough to hear him whisper in our ears that he has good things in store for us if we will stay close to his heart, listening for his truth, resting in the knowledge that he knows what he is doing. Just as God called out to the Israelites (who walked away from him regularly, I might add) through his prophet Jeremiah, he calls out to us: "'For I know the plans I have for you,' says the LORD. 'They are plans for good and not for disaster, to give you a future and a hope'" (Jer. 29:11).

He is saying the same to you. The thing that is making you crazy because you want it so much cannot fulfill you and give you what you want. Don't walk away from your Creator. Don't doubt his ability to give you what you need. The One who loves you best would like to hold you and remind you who he created you to be. He knows you inside and out. He knows exactly what you need. And he has good plans with your name written all over them. If I were you, I would stick around and find out what they are.

4

I Crave Apples and Other Things That Don't Satisfy Me

My nephew Drew recently had his first birthday. It was a high celebration including cousins, presents, and cake. Drew had his own full-size cake shaped like a cupcake, slathered with lemon frosting. This was placed in front of him to enjoy at his leisure. He was tentative at first, lightly dabbing at the yellow icing. But after the first taste, his eyes lit up with a hello-lovely-giant-cupcake look. Drew went to town, both hands fully engaged, as he began clutching handfuls of icing and placing them in his mouth. Not to be selfish, he offered some to passersby. Most declined, but Drew didn't seem to mind. It just meant more cake for him.

At some point in the cake fest, Drew began to slow down. He became subdued. His eyes were a bit glazed, and he seemed a little cake drunk, as my friend Barbie would say. My sister Jenny cleaned him off and sent him off to play. Until she noticed a mysterious redness spreading from the corners of his mouth, which prompted a call to the advice nurse. Clearly, you cannot have a truly great child's party unless some sort of medical care is required.

The wisdom of the ages was passed down by the advice nurse: watch the rash, apply cold compresses, and call back if it starts looking crazy. Have you ever tried to apply a cold compress to a one-year-old on a sugar high? It's not happening. And the whole "call back if it starts looking crazy" thing is like saying, "We don't really know what's wrong, but call back and we'll take a guess." So all that to say, Drew pulled through. The rash faded. He pepped up after he ran off some of the sugar, and the party continued to be a party.

Now I, personally, have never lit into a cake like that. I have limits. I have willpower and discipline and the knowledge that too much sugar is not good for your system. It also helps that I'm not that fond of cake. But if you put a box of dark-chocolate-covered peppermint cookies in front of me, I can polish off the entire box in under twelve minutes. Now, keep in mind that there are only sixteen cookies per box, so clearly I'm still within the legal limits of daily caloric intake for a woman . . . if I have only water for the rest of the week.

I tend to crave things that do me no good. Things that seem harmless, really. What is wrong with a chocolate mint cookie? (What was wrong with Eve's apple, for goodness' sake? It was full of fiber and vitamins.) Nothing, if it wasn't the key to one of my weaknesses: emotional eating. It is just one of my many weaknesses. I tend to crave things that make me feel good. (Hello, lovely chocolate.) But I also crave security, a sense of worth, love, stability, knowledge, and the list goes on and on. There are a number of apples the snake has lured me into biting into through the years.

I completely get Eve on this craving thing. There she was standing in front of the tree, and her mind had been changed. She was thinking, "I want to be like God. I want to know things. This apple is the key to all of that." It says in Genesis, "The woman was convinced. The fruit looked so fresh and delicious" (3:6). She rationalized that this fruit that God had told her to say no to should instead be a yes. She disregarded the truth of the Creator and locked in on the half-truths of a low-down, lying snake because she liked what he had to say better than what God had to say. And because she had a thing for fruit. The apple looked delicious. She tuned out the clear instruction of God and tuned in to the lie of the snake. She made what was wrong seem right in her own mind. What she wanted became her truth. Her desire became her path. And ours.

We have all been there a million times—standing at the foot of our personal forbidden tree, looking at the thing we crave, and in our mind convincing ourselves that this thing, whatever it may be at the moment, is *the* answer. If we can just sink our teeth into it, we will be full and satisfied and have all we ever needed. More often than not, we invite others into our dysfunction. We are able to rationalize it more when friends do it with us (e.g., if you get drunk by yourself, it's considered alcoholism, but if you get drunk with your friends, it's considered a party). If everyone is doing it, it must be right. Or not. As soon as Eve gets Adam snacking with her, both of them are down for the count.

We follow Eve's lead when we get our friends to eat, shop, spend, etc., with us. (You have no idea how many times I have tried to ply my husband with mint cookies to make up for my own overindulgence.) Then suddenly it's all okay. Everybody's doing it. Ever heard of the saying "Two wrongs don't make a right"? I think it may have been uttered first by God when he spotted a pair of apple cores in the garden. Why in the name of heaven do we keep falling for the lies of the snake and picking those apples? And why do we invite others to join us in our mess? Why are there affairs and alcoholism and binge eating and hoarding and thievery and bargain-shopping addictions? I believe it is because we are so desperate to be full.

Ever since the garden, humankind has been on a mad rampage to fill the creeping brokenness that pervades our lives. There is a yawning pit that continues to grow inside us. Our existence is not what it was originally designed to be. We are empty and long to be full. We flit from one apple to the next trying to get satisfied, and it's just not working. We want all the things God designed us for—relationship, wholeness, love, community, security, etc.—but we want them on our terms and we want them now.

When we shut out God's truth and the leading of his Spirit in our lives, we leave an immediate opening for the enemy of our souls to come in and wreak havoc. And the snake, with his trickery and his bent for destruction, knows what we want. (Remember that the snake could care less about what is good for us.) So he keeps up his empty diatribe, saying, "This is what you really want. It's not as bad as God says it is. It's really great. And come to think of it, why don't you invite all your friends to join you?" And we convince ourselves that he is right. The snake keeps feeding us lines, and we keep convincing ourselves that those apples are what he says they are. We let ourselves think that this time this apple is really what we want and what we need. We are sure of it.

The craziest part is that the "apple" we are craving usually tastes really good. Yummy. A lot like lemon icing, really. We go at it, two-fisted, giving it all we've got. (Drew has nothing on us!) Let's not fool ourselves. Eating the apple is usually really fun. You would think that if something were really bad for us we would lose all our bicuspids with the first bite, wouldn't you? But this is not usually the case. Mid-apple, we're usually feeling pretty good. The pump of adrenaline, the chocolate high, the spending rush, the illicit embrace all feel pretty great. We feel justified in our apple eating. We got what we wanted. Our appetite has been sated. Yeah for us!

We feel this way until 2.3 seconds after our apple munching comes to an end. That's when the stomachache kicks in, when our eyes are opened and we realize what we have actually done. We plunged ahead in an apple-eating frenzy, not thinking about the consequences to ourselves or to those around us. We took bite after deceptively delicious bite only to find ourselves a little subdued afterward, with a burgeoning rash.

The aftermath of the apple eating is always the worst (the hangover, the credit card bill, the loneliness after a one-night hookup). All we are left with is a nasty apple core and a gut full of regret. And where is that stupid snake? The one who spent so much time convincing us that this apple was all we ever needed to get full? He is long gone. And you know what? We're still not full. We just feel kind of sick and like we need a good herbal cleansing tea to set things right again. Or we go looking for another apple . . . because we think maybe the next one will be the one that really fills us up.

The truth is, there is no apple out there that can fill us. We can try any variety we want, but we'll still feel empty, mostly because we weren't made to be full of apples. We were made to be full of God's Spirit. The gaping hole in us, that soul emptiness, was meant to be filled with a relationship with our Creator. We can go crazy and fill up on a variety of substitutes, but we won't feel full. God is the only One who can offer us peace and joy and wholeness and a love that satiates the irrational hunger that seems to overwhelm us at times.

The beginning of Acts 17:28 says, "For in him we live and move and exist." It is that simple . . . and that complicated.

We have a deep need, and it can be met only in God. In fact, without God we can't truly live. Our fullness doesn't come on our terms but instead when we recognize that we need God more than anything else. Are you standing at the foot of your proverbial tree, reaching for a luscious-looking apple, convincing yourself that this is the one and this time you will feel full? Stop. Don't eat it. It isn't the one. No matter how many apples we try, it will never be the one. The sooner we realize that the better. Better yet, we should realize that he is the One. God is the only One who can satiate the great hunger that seems to be overtaking our lives. And more importantly, it is his heart's desire to fill our lives with his presence. He would like to fill us to overflowing with his love, mercy, and grace. And there is nothing as satisfying as that. Not even a giant cupcake.

5

I Think I Need Some Fig Leaves to Cover Up My Shame

Being a church planter's wife has its perks and its drawbacks. I get to be married to Scott—life with him is an adventure. On the other hand, I am often called upon to do things I may not feel comfortable doing. As a result, I often humiliate myself in a variety of ways. In the words of Inigo Montoya of *The Princess Bride* fame, "Humiliations galore!" And even though we have been church planting for almost six years now, the ways I shame myself are fresh and new each time. I don't like to do it the same way twice.

One particularly memorable moment happened when I was called upon to lead worship last year. I told Scott, "Please don't have me lead worship. Bad things happen when I lead worship. People can't feel the Lord's presence. I quench the Spirit." I like to use church-ese when I plead with Scott. I think it sounds more holy. This particular Sunday we had two guest speakers. It seems to add more pressure when people who don't know that you are an awkward worship leader show up for church. My sister Jenny was backing me up with harmony, and our friend Justin was on guitar. Scott was playing the congas. We started singing and gingerly made our way through our song lineup. So far so good. Our visitors were worshiping along with us. Until we got to the bridge of "Here I Am to Worship." I spoke the next words we would be singing.

"I'll never know how much it cost . . ."

Then I inhaled, taking a deep breath before singing, which resulted in my sucking spit down my windpipe. Do you know what happens when you suck spit down your windpipe? Instead of singing, "I'll never know how much it cost," you make the sound "Cack!" Do you know what that sound does when you are leading worship? It quenches the Spirit. It also scares your sister, who is harmonizing with you, so she stops singing altogether and places a hand on your back to determine if she needs to give you the Heimlich. It confuses the guitar player and brings shame on your conga-playing husband. And it causes visitors to avert their praises to God and start praying on your behalf instead. I know this because I asked Char (one of the guest speakers who is now a dear friend despite the "cacking") what she thought of that breath-taking interlude, and she said she immediately began praying for me. See? A distinct Spirit quench admitted by a stranger. Jenny quickly took up the melody line, and I limped on through the song in a breathy, halfhearted voice because I sincerely believed I had injured my vocal cords. I died a little inside that day . . . as I always do when I embarrass myself. There was nothing I could do to hide my shame. I had broadcast it through the loudspeakers.

I have always had an aversion to embarrassment and to revealing my imperfections. And this is just your everyday embarrassment that has no bearing on my relationship with God. Don't even get me started about how humiliating it is when I have to talk about my sins and the remorse and guilt I feel over them. I would rather have you poke my eyes out or subject me to water torture than reveal them to you or anyone else, for that matter. Because now we are not just talking about that time I "cacked" during worship; we are talking about how I've let God and everyone else down. That is more than just embarrassing; it's shameful. I will do most anything to keep from feeling ashamed. Shame is that wretched oh-sweet-lordy-the-cat-is-out-of-the-bag feeling that sweeps over us and leaves us feeling clammy and nauseated.

Shame is a reaction to seeing ourselves for who we are when we have done something wrong. We are sinners, one and all. (I know that word isn't politically correct, but let's just call it like it is.) All have fallen short of the glory of God. All we like sheep have gone astray. We have all embarrassed ourselves in front of God. He created us for rightness and relationship with him, and we have cornered the market on wrongness and selfishness. When we catch a glimpse of ourselves, post-sin, our eyes are opened. We feel exposed. Naked. Ashamed. And we immediately start looking around for some fig leaves. Now, fig leaves are pretty big. But there is nothing that can cover up that sense of vulnerability when we are found out.

The first thing Adam and Eve did when they felt shame was to cover up their privates with fig leaves, which is an interesting choice, I think. I wonder how long it was after that last bite of apple that they realized their most vulnerable parts were on display. Why hadn't they noticed they were naked before? And why did they feel compelled to cover up their privates? There seemed to be a distinct lack of concern for all other body parts such as elbows and necks. Maybe it was because for the first time they recognized themselves in all their humanness. I wonder how that cover-up conversation went.

"Adam, I think we better cover up our nether regions before God comes around this afternoon. We wouldn't want him to see us naked."

"I agree, Eve. I think a fig leaf skirt will do the trick. That'll fool him for sure."

I can imagine the hurried gathering of leaves and the quick sewing job as a sense of panic pervaded the air. "Hurry! He's coming." There's a lot of fidgeting. The fig leaves don't drape well. They will be found out for sure. It seems silly, doesn't it? How did they think they could cover up what they had done with greenery? I don't know. How do we?

We think we are far more sophisticated than Adam and Eve with their paltry fig leaves when we come face-to-face with our sin nature. We have other methods that we use when our sins are found out. We usually take to lying. To ourselves. To God. To others. We cover up our sins with half-truths and poor excuses. We say things like, "Well, it's really not sinning. I had to do what is right for me." Or, "How was I supposed to know it would end up like this? God should have been more clear about what he wanted from me." Or, "It seemed like the right thing to do at the time."

Cover-ups. We're pretty good at them. We are well practiced in hiding our faults. Despite our best efforts, our cover-ups are about as effective as Eve's fig leaf couture. God sees us for who we are. Broken. Exposed. Sinful. Sorry. Vulnerable. Every one of us. None of us can figure out a way to get God to look past who we truly are in all our humanness. It doesn't matter how well we can sew fig leaves or try to hide our shame. He knows us. The time we figure out we are naked and ashamed is about two seconds too late. He's coming. He's coming! This is the terrifying part. But you should know it is also the best part.

Here we are, naked in our wrongdoing, freaking out, trying to cover up. But it is only when we recognize ourselves for who we are (sinners) that we can let God begin to do his work in us. Standing in the light of his glorious rightness, we see ourselves for who we really are. Are you a wreck? A mess? A screwup? A sinner? A complete and total reprobate? Excellent. Are you broken? Hurt? Dysfunctional? Embarrassed by your sins? Perfect. This is the moment, the one when we are covered in fig leaves and guilt, when we realize how much we need the One who is on his way. The One who is longing for a real relationship with us. The One who loves us mess and all. When we get caught, we can know two things: (1) we are not perfect, and (2) we are about to receive an opportunity for grace to begin a work in our hearts. It is that simple. So if you find yourself, even now, sewing a skirt of remorse and shame, put your needle down. Wipe your tears. And get ready. His grace is on its way. This is just the beginning of your journey toward freedom.

I Want to Hide from God

One day when my son Addison was around three years old, something terrible happened. It was early morning, and I didn't know he was hiding in my room when I got out of the shower. As I was reaching for my clothes, I noticed him huddled in the corner, eyes wide, full of fear. I recognized the look in his eyes since I have the same look when I see myself without clothing. I screamed and dropped to the ground, hoping for full coverage. He screamed back. I can only pray that that image was not seared into his young mind, scarring him for life.

Public nakedness is something most of us are not comfortable with. This could be because we know that if we go out in public with no clothes on, we will end up in handcuffs trying to explain ourselves to a judge. But from the beginning in the garden, nakedness was the desired state. Nothing to hide. No shame. Literally. If nakedness was the enforced dress code today, there would be a lot less ego. And a lot more of us would be doing push-ups and passing up chocolate chip cookies. Mostly because cellulite is so unattractive in broad daylight. But Adam and Eve had never experienced this fear of being completely exposed. As soon as Eve took that bite, that all shifted. And after sewing themselves some coverings of leaves, they had a new revelation: fig leaves were not going to cut it. They were going to need an entire forest to hide themselves. It says in Genesis that when they heard God walking in the garden, they took to the trees. It tends to be what most of us do when we have a fear of being exposed.

When I was growing up, I attended some youth camps. I went because there were boys there and I liked boys a whole lot. But I also went because I loved Jesus and I knew he was there too. Some of the speakers were fantastic, pointing us Christward with their words and their passion for his grace and mercy. But some of the speakers scared us to death because they would go old-school and call you out. "Calling you out" meant they would point at you and tell you something about yourself and your relationship with God in front of the entire camp. They would say something like, "You in the red shirt! God wants you to know he loves you and he wants you to quit running away from him!" It seemed as if they were peering into your very soul. I often thought it would be kinder for the speaker to motion people aside *after* the service and secretly slip them a note with their sins written on it so they could all be kept on the down low. Why all the public humiliation? The air was always charged with nervous energy and the smell of teenage fear. Two hundred kids caught in the terrible grip of puberty were all fervently praying, "Dear God, don't let him pick me next!"

I was petrified. I always kept my head down, avoiding eye contact, pretending I was praying, hoping my fake holiness would throw them off. The process was like Russian roulette. You never knew who was going to be next. Of course, when someone other than you was called out, there was a great sense of relief, and the silent praises of hundreds of kids would shoot up to the heavens, saying, "Thank God it wasn't me!" We got through the service by the skin of our teeth because the truth was we all had things to hide in our lives. Things we were ashamed of. Sins that troubled us. And for the most part, we wanted those things to stay hidden. That is why we hadn't exposed them ourselves. But it seems that secrecy is not God's modus operandi. He prefers the calling-out method over hiding. He seems to like things out in the open. We know this because it says so in Genesis: "The Lord God called to Adam, 'Where are you?' He replied, 'I heard you, so I hid. I was afraid because I was naked'" (3:9–10).

God is calling out Adam. You can almost hear him. "Hey, Adam! Where are you?"

I don't think that Adam and Eve were the best hide-and-seekers of all time. Obviously, God knows they are cowering behind the oak trees. Why does he ask Adam where he is? Maybe because God wants Adam to recognize where he is. Maybe he wants Adam to realize what he is doing and why he is doing it.

I can just see Adam glancing around at his whereabouts and calling back to God, "We freaked out when we heard you coming. I'm in the trees and scared because I just realized I don't have any pants on." Adam realizes he is not where he is supposed to be or who he is supposed to be. He is supposed to be strolling in the garden with his Maker. He is supposed to be completely comfortable in his own skin. He is supposed to be sinless. But instead he finds himself a sinner, scared out of his mind at what is about to happen, camping out in the bushes, hoping God will pass him by.

Something else terrible happened when Eve bit into the apple. Fear was introduced into the world—mind-numbing, heart-pounding fear. Up until this point, Adam and Eve had nothing to be afraid of, no reason at all to be scared. But when they heard God walking in the garden, they were petrified. They had disobeyed, and now they were going to see how everything would go down.

We have all been there. Afraid. Hearing God come near. Asking us what in the world we have been thinking and why we are hiding from him. It is a scary place to be. Terrifying, really. But here is the thing. There is no help in the trees for Adam and Eve. All they have on hand is their fig leaf skirts and their fear. And just like them, there is no help for us either when we stay hidden, keeping our hearts and lives from God, tucking away our sins, and peering at him from behind leafy branches. When we stick to the trees, when we harbor our sins in secret, we remain separated from the only One who can help us, the only One who has a solution for our dilemma. When God calls us out, even with our knees knocking and our palms sweating, we have to come out. I don't think it's a coincidence that the Greek word most often used in the New Testament for church is *ecclesia*, or "called-out" ones. God has been calling us out by name, one at a time, since the time of Eden. He knows we can be changed only when we come out of hiding and into his presence.

"George, where are you?" "Abby, for goodness' sake, what are you doing?" "Gwen, don't make me come in there after you!"

The list of names goes on and on, yours and mine included. God loves you, plain and simple. He longs for you to be done with your hiding, with your fear, with your cowering. He would like to get on with it. "It" being pouring out his mercy and grace on you in spite of your wrongdoing. "It" being reminding you that he knows you inside and out and that he would like to be a part of your life. "It" being forgiving you and showing you that he is the One with the answers and the healing for your pain. He knows where you are, and he is calling you out even now. And there is just one thing to do. Come out with your hands up and find out how much the God of the universe loves you.

7

I Would Rather Not Take Responsibility for My Actions

Our house is rarely quiet. The noise that emanates from three boys ages ten and under is ebullient at best and deafening at worst. Scott and I do not understand when people say things like, "Our kids played quietly together this afternoon." Clearly, their children are not human. Or maybe they are just not boys. In our house, it is usually loud with an occasional breaking of the sound barrier. Sometimes more than the sound barrier gets broken.

Quite often I hear an out-of-the-ordinary loud noise, a bump or a crash or both simultaneously. This is followed by anxious whispering or heated arguing. At this point, I follow the sounds of mayhem even though I know I may be saddened by what I find. I am part bloodhound, part Hercule Poirot when it comes to finding out the wrongdoings of my children. In due time, I come upon an item, like a lamp or a chair, that is broken or maimed or lying in some unrecognizable state. And with an air of serenity and calm, I yell, "Who did this?" I want to know because someone is going down. The boys know this, and they don't want Mommy to take them down, so they try to form an alliance of silence. They can see the displeasure on my face. The furrowed eyebrows. The downturn of the mouth. The frantic eye tic. And they know whatever is coming is not going to be pretty.

I usually deal out a joint punishment. "Everyone go to your room." At this point, the little one, Addison, cracks, because to him going to his room is equivalent to jail time. He starts to rat out his older brothers.

"Well, they were chasing me, and then they broke it." This brings cries of disbelief from the older two, Jack and Will.

"We did not! We were just sitting there, and he knocked it over. We didn't do anything."

"They said a monster was going to eat me, so I had to run."

"We were just doing our homework, quietly and politely."

There is usually a lot of finger pointing and some fibbing and some weeping. Blaming each other is one of my children's all-time favorite pastimes. Each one comes up with a creative story as to why it could not possibly have been him. Eventually, we come to the truth, which usually includes some fault on each child's part. And then we are back to sending everyone to his room. Jail time, as it were. Just in case you thought the only ones who struggle with owning up to their sins in our house are the kids, it's time to think again. They come by it honestly. They are just like their mother.

Blaming other people for things I've done seems much easier than owning up to the fact that I slipped up. I really don't enjoy taking responsibility for my actions. On a scale of one to ten, ten being the most you can hate doing something, I'm a fourteen and a half when it comes to owning up to my mistakes. I hate being found out. I hate having someone point out that I am wrong. And I hate having to admit to the fact that, yes, it is me. I am the one to blame. It just leaves a bad taste in my mouth.

Now, I have no trouble at all letting you know if I think you have wronged me. We can get that right out in the open. "Last week, when you did that thing, it was terrible. Ripped me right to shreds. It really did. I hope you can make it right. I'm not sure you can, but I'll see if I can work up some forgiveness for you." But if, by chance, the tables are turned, and you come to me, heartbroken, wounded by something I have done, and say, "Why on earth did you do this?" I would maybe feign some shock. "What? No! How can that be? I did that to you? I am usually so much nicer than that. Maybe it was someone else who looked and sounded like me. Clearly, you were dealing with a robot imposter, a pod person who looked like me but really wasn't me. I would never hurt you on purpose. Are we good now?"

Now, what I'm going to say next may come as a shock. I have been wrong a lot. And even more shocking, I know you have been wrong a lot too. Unfortunately, being wrong just comes naturally to us. To some more naturally than others. But like it or not, we all have moments in our lives when we have to own up to our wrongs, when we have to look someone in the eye and say, "Begging your pardon, but I seem to have a problem with sin, and I'm sorry that some of my sins have affected you." It's so awkward. But here is the thing. Most of the time the person you are owning up to, usually someone you care about or spend time with, knows already. They know you have sins and that you've hurt them, and they want two things from you: (1) they want you to admit you did in fact do this wrong thing, and (2) they want you to deal with the results of it. And we know from our sister Eve that this is never easy to do.

I can just imagine Adam and Eve standing that evening in the garden, eyes downcast, digging in the dirt with their toes as God begins to question them. "'Who told you that you were naked?' the LORD God asked. 'Have you eaten the fruit I commanded you not to eat?'" (Gen. 3:11). And then it comes: the repentant heart, the weeping, the owning up to the apple eating. Nope, guess not. It's more like finger pointing and shameless blaming. It appears that Adam and Eve didn't like to accept responsibility for their actions any more than I do. "'Yes,' Adam admitted, 'but it was the woman you gave me who brought me the fruit, and I ate it.' Then the LORD God asked the woman, 'How could you do such a thing?' 'The serpent tricked me,' she replied. 'That's why I ate it'" (Gen. 3:12–13).

Adam quickly blamed Eve, and Eve in turn passed the blame on to the snake. My dad also likes to point out that Adam said, "The woman *you* gave me," including God in his blame game as well. When all else fails, why not blame God? Maybe it will work for you. It didn't work for Adam. Usually, God has a pretty good idea who the culprit in the situation is, he being omniscient and all.

We don't want to own up to our sins because we don't want to deal with the punishment afterward. Whether we are a five-year-old caught with our hand in the cookie jar or a bank executive caught embezzling large wads of cash, we would like to get away with as much as we can and not have to deal with the consequences of our actions. That's where blame comes in. When confronted with the truth that we are sinners, often our natural response is to start pointing fingers. We blame our marriage. We blame the lousy economy. We blame our parents and our upbringing. We blame the fact that we are broke or the fact that we are rich. We blame our culture. We blame our lack of education. We blame our past relationships or our lack of past relationships. And when all else fails, we blame God.

But this will get us nowhere. Not with God. Not with each other. The crazy part is that even if we don't own up to our wrongdoing, we will still have to deal with the consequences of our actions. One way or another our souls bend and twist under the weight of what we've done. We may be able to keep our mouths shut, but our lives will shout out the results of the choices we have made. It says so in the Word. The apostle Paul reminds us in Galatians 6:7–8, "Don't be misled. Remember that you can't ignore God and get away with it. You will always reap what you sow! Those who live only to satisfy their own sinful desires will harvest the consequences of decay and death."

Well, now that sounds terrible, doesn't it? Harvesting decay and death? That's not the life we are looking to live. But if we choose to blame others rather than accept responsibility for what we have done, that is exactly what we will get. A life that is dead on the vine. No growth. No hope. No future. Well, then all is lost. Unless . . . there is some great unimaginable grace that has been set aside for us. And apparently, there is. John, the one Jesus loved, knew this and laid it out for us in 1 John 1:8–9: "If we say we have no sin, we are only fooling ourselves and refusing to accept the truth. But if we confess our sins to him, he is faithful and just to forgive us and to cleanse us from every wrong."

And there it is. Confession. Truth telling. Soul baring. The antithesis of blame. Blame will get us nowhere fast. It will leave us digging our toes in the dirt, eyes downcast, fooling ourselves as we try telling God that it's everyone else's fault. But when we own up to our junk, when we come before the most high God, place a palm on our chest, and say, "It was me. I did it. I messed up," something amazing and mind-blowing happens. He is faithful and just to forgive us our sins. Not just the sins from last Thursday or two years ago but each and every wrong thing we have ever done. And you know what that means, don't you? It means we are about to be free. That thing that has been haunting us, that we have been dodging and hoping won't catch up with us, is now out in the open. Its power is diminished. Now that we have owned it, help is on the way. Because when we turn our faces heavenward and raise a hand and say, "I did it and I'm sorry," God gets to say to us, "I know it and I love you." Our confession allows God to do what he does best. Forgive us.

So you have a choice. Eve's way. Run, hide, and blame others and find a life of death and decay, harvesting what you plant each day. Or you can try it God's way. Confess. Tell him your deepest, darkest secrets. Tell him what holds you down, the weight of all those wrongs you have been carrying with you. Tell him what you did. That you have been wrong, and even though you have been denying it all along, you are owning all of it now. And you will run smack into an endless supply of grace, mercy, and forgiveness flowing from the One who loves you best. It's a tough choice, I know. But go with your gut. I think you'll get it right.

8

I Have at Least One Enemy

My brother, Chris, and I used to hunt garter snakes on the hillside below our house when we were growing up. Chris was much better at it than I was. He was fearless and fast, scooping them up out of the dust and weeds. I would hold them and let them wind around my fingers like reptilian brass knuckles. Chris often used them to scare my mom or my sisters. But my sister Jenny was by far the best one to scare. She is a jumper. Loud noises, quick movements, or surprises are her undoing. When we were kids, Chris and I used to lie in wait for her outside the bathroom door, and when she would come out, we would yell, "Boo!" Every time, she'd issue a loud shriek accompanied by a wild windmilling of the arms. She would usually konk us on the head with whatever she had on hand. I seem to recall being taken down by a Goody brush one time. But the momentary pain was always worth the enormity of her reaction. We couldn't help ourselves. We liked to make Jenny jump.

One of the best scares I ever got out of Jenny was when I was visiting Mom and Dad and Jenny at Gordon-Conwell Theological Seminary. Jenny was studying there, and my parents were the ministers in residence. We were driving down a country road in Massachusetts and saw a beautiful old red barn rising up out of a lovely flower-filled meadow. Mom pulled over so we could take a picture of it. As Jenny and I made our way toward the fence in front of the barn, I passed by a worn-out bike tire, split in half and coiled on the ground. As Jenny followed me past it, I screamed, "Snake!" Jenny, catching a glimpse of the winding rubber out of the corner of her eye, screamed a scream that would have done a banshee proud. When she realized it was a bike tire and not a snake, she was not happy. Nope. She probably wished she had a Goody brush to swing at me. But one of the other things I love about Jenny is that she is also a good sport. She was such a good sport that I have a lovely picture of her holding up the bike tire snake in front of a weathered red barn. Classic.

Unfortunately for us, the snake in the garden was not as benign as a mangled bike tire lying by the side of the road. After the fall, he and Eve were no longer on speaking terms. He made it his mission to take her and all of her kind down. Cursed by God and hated by humankind, the snake has been up to no good ever since. And while we may think that snakes that hide under rocks are creepy, their spiritual counterpart is even creepier. Ever since he got the boot from the garden, he has done all within his power to destroy the ones whom God loves. That would be all of humanity. He is not some figment of the imagination. He is real. And I think it is safe to say that he is ticked off. He has done his best to promote evil and selfishness and all things underhanded in our world. Our demise is his delight. He is a sicko. That's for sure.

Jesus's disciple Peter knew this all too well. He warned the believers of the early church, "Be careful! Watch out for attacks from the Devil, your great enemy. He prowls around like a roaring lion, looking for some victim to devour" (1 Peter 5:8).

Now, I have enough struggles on my own without worrying about someone trying to take me out with my weaknesses and blind spots. Especially a snake. I am of the school of folks who run away wild-eyed and freaked out when coming up against him or one of his tricks. According to Peter, this is the wrong approach entirely. This is not what Peter advises his readers to do. He doesn't say, "At first sighting of the gnarly beast, run screaming like a girl to the church nearest you." Which would be my first thought. He goes on to say in 1 Peter 5:9, "Take a firm stand against him, and be strong in your faith. Remember that Christians all over the world are going through the same kind of suffering you are." Peter is in essence saying, "Don't be caught off guard by him. Stand your ground and remember whom you believe in. Whenever you feel alone, remember that you are not the only one he is messing with." Peter is not exhorting the church to bring about fear and panic. He is telling them to remember whose side they are on. Whose side we are on. This battle is not just between Eve's offspring and the snake. It never has been and it never will be. Peter knew that he could stand firm because God and all that he did through Jesus's amazing work on the cross defeated death and hell. He knew he could stand firm because the One who redeemed him lives. And in the end, Jesus is the one who wins, not the snake.

I remember one of my theology professors asking us, on a scale of one to ten, how much power we thought God had. We said ten of course. We were a savvy bunch. Then he posed the same question about the devil. On a scale of one to ten, how much power did we think he had. There were a variety of answers. I gave him a solid four, if I remember correctly. Then our professor said, "In the presence of God, the devil has no power. You have just given him more power in your minds than he deserves." It was an eye-opener, really. It put things in perspective. If we stand on our own against the enemy of our soul, like Eve did in the garden, we can expect shaky results at best. But if we invite God into those weak and sin-darkened areas of our lives where the enemy does his dirty work, all the enemy can do is run.

The snake knows this. Even if he defeats every one of us in a thousand ways, he still cannot defeat the Creator, the One who formed the world in his hands and all the beings that live in it. The enemy is living on borrowed time, and he is trying his best to wreak as much havoc as he can in what little time he has. He wants to take us all out at the knees with doubt and worry and fear and disbelief. If he can get us scared, cowering in the corner, afraid to call out to the One who can save us, he wins the round. But I love that Peter doesn't play that game. He doesn't buy into the idea that we are going down anytime soon. Because he knows whom he believes in. He knows who wins in the end. We can stand firm because someone else is doing the fighting. Someone far more powerful than the snake has our back. And while the snake may be running amok here and there, he knows that his day is coming. That is why he is so frantic, so wound up. He may barter with lies and deal in shoddy half-truths, trying to sway us to his point of view, but he knows the truth.

When Jesus took our shame, our moral poverty, and our endless mess-ups and nailed them to the cross, the keys to death and destruction were snatched from the snake's slithery hold. He lost. While that victory may feel far off to us as we struggle against the snake's wily ways, we can hold on tight and know the truth. In the battle of dark and light, the wars of good versus evil, God always wins. Always. And in the end, the snake will be reduced to nothing more than an overblown tire on the side of the road. He will have no more power over the ones God loves than a puff of hot air as his evil plans are laid to waste.

So the next time you are struggling, caught up in fear, feeling defeated, and someone screams, "Snake!" take a deep breath and remember who is on your side. Remember whose love and grace are grounding you, remember whose mercy and hope are strengthening your bones, and stand your ground. Remember that you are not alone in your fight against the snake and his twisted truth. Hundreds, thousands, millions, even, all over the world are standing with you, journeying with you as you follow after the Christ. And most importantly, remember that on a dark Friday long ago on the hill of the skull, the One who fought the fight against evil won. Hands down. He pinned our sins to a tree, gave the snake what he had coming, and rose on a bright morning so that we would never have to be without him again. His love conquered all for us and made a way back into the Father's warm presence for us, and we can rest assured that he is on our side. No matter what the battle or struggle you are facing, fast and furious, slow and monotonous, he's got you and he always wins. And that is a good thing to remember.

9

I Feel Really Sad That There Is Pain in Childbirth

Birthing a child is one of the most breathtaking experiences known to womankind. Literally. It just sucks your breath right out of you. Now, I need to pause here and say that there are many views on the best way to birth a child. There are those in favor of natural childbirth, and there are those in favor of some drugs to help with the pain. For the record, an epidural does not alleviate all birthing pain. Don't think that any of us mothers have escaped the harshness of Eve's curse, drugs or not. An epidural is merely an aid in the birthing process, a mere window of relaxation in a veritable five-year, pain-filled process. The pain in childbirth starts around week six of pregnancy, beginning with intermittent nausea and heartburn, and continues on through the last trimester, when you are as large as a bus and your joints creak under the added weight of the baby (and the copious amounts of soft-serve ice cream you have consumed). It lasts through the child's fourth year of life, when you are still trying to cast off the remnants of sleep deprivation. So "painfree" childbirth is clearly a misnomer.

I had my second son, Will, at a hospital with one of the highest rates of epidural use on the East Coast. I took this as a clear sign that God knew me and loved me. When I went into labor, our first stop in the hospital was the triage area, where a nurse hooked me up to a baby heart rate monitor and recorded my contractions. After a few minutes of hard contractions, I motioned the nurse over. "When can I have my epidural?" She raised an eyebrow and said, "Ma'am, we have to admit you to the hospital first." Whatever. Obviously, she needed to get a move on and get this thing done. Didn't she know what was coming next?

A very real palpable fear is realized by women everywhere in the course of labor. That is the fear that soon they will be experiencing the near impossible scenario of a child being brought into the world in a rather incomprehensible manner. During hard labor, many a husband has lost the use of all his fingers when his hand has been crushed in his wife's gorilla-like grasp. Clear-thinking women have been known to throw cups of gingerly offered ice chips on the ground and howl. So let's not get caught up in the details and get lost in the bureaucratic red tape here. Let's get this girl some drugs, people, before something happens that we will all regret. Clearly, things are not as they should be, with the pain and all.

Childbirth, the joy and miracle of it, was never intended to be accompanied by pain. But when Eve walked away from the life God had created for her, she had to deal with the consequences of her actions. The natural process of birth, which should have been breathtaking with exhilaration, became gut-wrenching . . . in a very real sense. With one bite, everything that was good and right in Eve's life began to break down. Every aspect of her heart, soul, mind, and body was affected by the choice she made. (Birthing included.) Every corner of her life became less than it was created to be as sin seeped in, coloring the edges and hardening the corners. Eve's life was broken. There would now be pain where there had never been pain before, physically, emotionally, and spiritually. This is the legacy that is handed down to us.

So we deal with the consequences not only of Eve's choices but also of our own daily choices. We live less than perfect lives that show all the signs of coming apart at the seams. Even on our best days, we can't get past the fact that life hurts. Not one of us gets through this process unscathed. In fact, most of us look for a way to make it better. More than a few of us are found yelling, "When can I get my epidural?" or, "Is there a pill I can take to make this easier?" When we realize there are no easy solutions to real living, we try to anesthetize ourselves. We try to fashion a life with the least amount of pain.

Some of us try to bury the pain under guilty pleasures, self-soothing, and pacifying ourselves. When life begins to feel broken, we go shopping or indulge in a new relationship or eat our way through a bakery. When the good feelings wear off and the despair begins to creep back in, we simply repeat the process, committing to a lifestyle of overindulgence to survive. Others of us respond by trying to control our surroundings. We figure that if we can make our world look like we think it should then we will feel better. We organize ourselves into corners and negotiate impossible to-do lists. When we can't control our environment, we try to control other people, placing high hurdles in their paths and holding them to standards they can never attain. Still others of us try to perfect ourselves, thinking that if we can patch ourselves up with self-improvement books and breathing exercises we will lessen the pain of real living. Or some of us do all of these things. Like me. As you can imagine, living with me is no walk in the park.

But the wildest part is that with all the pain and brokenness of this life, we have the audacity to think we can fix ourselves. We turn ourselves inside out looking for peace, for deliverance, for clarity, when as far as I can tell, we don't have a whole lot of peace, deliverance, or clarity on hand. We try to set ourselves free when we don't have the ability to do so. Just like there is no way on this green earth that I could give myself an epidural, there is no way we can bring healing about in our own lives. We would be crazy to think otherwise.

There is only one person who can fix the brokenness in us, and that is the One who knit us together in our mother's belly in the first place, the One who knows our every thought and calls us his own. He can bring peace into our lives and clarity into our minds. We have to rely on the Healer to mend our brokenness. In Psalm 147:3, the psalmist says, "He heals the brokenhearted, binding up their wounds." He alone can take the pieces of our lives and fashion them into something authentic and beautiful. I don't think it was happenstance that Jesus was a carpenter when he came to earth. His entire purpose for coming revolves around restoration. He restores the wandering child to his loving Father, the lost sheep to the Shepherd. The blind receive sight, the deaf can hear, the lame can do a funky dance of joy in the Creator's presence. Redemption is his forte. He is the God who can make something out of nothing and restore the broken pieces of our lives to wholeness. He is the only One who can.

Even though we are living with the consequences of Eve's choices, we are not stuck in this place of pain with no one to help us. We are not alone in our quest to bandage the wounds that are bleeding so profusely in our lives. The Creator cannot stand it when his creation is hurting. This is why he has made a way of healing for us. He has formed a path that leads to a place of peace when the circumstances of life have left us begging for more than a paltry glass of ice chips. Jesus came so that in spite of all the heartache and the missteps in our lives, he can fashion a life for us that sings of peace and hope. He came to do that for you. He came to do that for me. So don't be afraid if there is an area (or every single area) of your life that you can't seem to manage or fix or put back together. This is what the journey of freedom is all about. Putting your heart and soul back in the hands of the One who created you. So place your life in the capable hands of the Creator and let him do what only he can. Make all things new. No epidural required.

10

I Have the Eden Gene

Just yesterday when I got up from writing, I found that I was stuck to my chair. Literally. As I stood up, there was a sound of suction breaking. When I reached back and touched the back of my pants, it all became clear. It was gum. How gum had found its way to the seat of my pants I do not know. Obviously, with three boys in my house, there is always the possibility of some type of unusual substance finding its way into my life. A deep sense of "Are you kidding me?" welled up within me. Here I was with gum on my pants surrounded by scribbled notes, half-filled cups of cold coffee, and a truckload of clean clothes waiting to be folded. I'm pretty sure what I really needed at that moment was a lounge chair and a fruity drink served to me on a white-sand beach in Hawaii. That is the life I was made for. My own personal Eden.

The chasm between the life I live and the Eden-like existence I long for is large, to put it mildly. I love living in the heart of the Silicon Valley, but I was designed for the beach-bum lifestyle. I was made for afternoons filled with body surfing and building sand castles with the boys, for moonlit strolls with Scott and the thrum of the waves on the shore. I was created with a hunger in my soul that can only be sated by ripe mangoes and chocolate-covered macadamia nuts. It's a fantasy, really. I know I would still have laundry piled on my bed in Hawaii. But I can pretend my laundry would smell like guava juice and a live-in maid would put it away for me. This fantasy is highly preferable to, say, being stuck to my chair by a wad of bubble gum.

Real life can be disheartening sometimes. Whenever I am struck down by hard things, I tend to send a complaint heavenward that sounds something like, "This is not how life is supposed to be!" or even more eloquently, "Are you kidding me?" I wish someone was kidding me. Whenever a friend is leveled by sickness or family strife or marital problems, I yell out on their behalf too. "No! No! No! It wasn't supposed to go this way." Or here's a good one: "What in the world?!" I know it in my gut. You know it in yours. Life was not meant to be like this. Disruptive. Annoying. Devastating. Distracting. Guilt ridden. Fractured. Somewhere, somehow, lingering deep within our gene pool is the knowledge we were originally designed for a chaos-free life.

It's as if Eve, all those long years ago, harbored a memory of Eden in her bones. The ease and grace of a perfect life worked its way into the very fabric of her being. And even though she had to leave the garden, she still carried the taste of it in her mouth and the feel of it in her soul. It seems that down through the millennia a latent gene buried deep within her DNA has been passed on to us. I call it the Eden gene. Even though we never stepped foot in Eden, we hunger for it, this place of untainted relationships and perfect provision. This

Eden gene, however metaphorical it may be, holds within it the memory of what life was meant to be like. Fair. Gracious. Hopeful. Authentic. Generous. Sacred. Joyful. Even though we have never seen a perfect day, let alone a perfect life, we long for it. We recognize that there is a whole lot of wrong going on every day that we were not meant for. Sickness. Hatred. Confusion. Fear. Death. God didn't create humankind for tragedy and ugliness. He created us for good living, loving relationships, wholeness, and free pineapple.

With all the tragedy found in day-to-day living, it is easy to see how one could succumb to mind-numbing depression and the need for strong liquor. Most of us, when faced with trials and heartaches, do not want to learn powerful life lessons. Nope. We want out. We want to escape. We want Hawaii or a café in Paris or a fast canoe on the Amazon that will whisk us away to paradise. We want the verdant garden and the perfect order it offered. We want the harmonious relationships and the free fruit. We want Eden, for crying out loud. Sounds pretty good, doesn't it?

But here is the kicker. Get a tissue because this is rough stuff you are about to read. God is no longer offering us Eden, no matter how much we wish he was. He is not offering us a life of perfection. He is offering us salvation. He is offering us forgiveness. He is offering us hope and a new future. But as far as I can tell, Eden is not back on the table. I've looked through many Scripture passages, hoping for some kind of loophole, but nowhere in the Bible does it say, "And now since you believe in God, you can have the life you always dreamed of." Or, "Now that you have decided to follow Jesus, you can reenter the state of bliss that Adam and Eve once lived in." Apparently, a perfect life and a trouble-free world are no longer available to us this side of heaven. Even with the presence of Christ and his salvation in our lives, our world remains imperfect. Once sin entered the world, everything was altered. It says in Romans 8:20–25:

> Against its will, everything on earth was subjected to God's curse. All creation anticipates the day when it will join God's children in glorious freedom from death and decay. For we know that all creation has been groaning as in the pains of childbirth right up to the present time. And even we Christians, although we have the Holy Spirit within us as a foretaste of future glory, also groan to be released from pain and suffering. We, too, wait anxiously for that day when God will give us our full rights as his children, including the new bodies he has promised us. Now that we are saved, we eagerly look forward to this freedom. For if you already have something, you don't need to hope for it. But if we look forward to something we don't have yet, we must wait patiently and confidently.

Clearly, God has a plan. Everything will be made right. When we get to heaven, everything will be as it should be. No more sorrow or pain or death. No more cellulite or taxes or gossip. Bodies will be restored, and we will be released from all suffering and given a place of honor as God's children. All we have to do is wait patiently and confidently for what he has promised us. There is only one problem with this passage. God forgot that we, his fallen creation, are terrible at being patient. We don't like waiting. It takes so long. It's not that we don't think God's plan is great. It's just that we are ready for a little relief now. The end of time seems so distant. Couldn't we have just a little perfect here on earth?

Into this place of wavering and discontent slithers the insipid snake, prodding and poking us with his words. "Wow, are you really going to wait that long to get the life you want?" or, "Seems like God is going to let you suffer a lot before you get to live the good life," or, "Why don't you make your life the way you want it now?" This line worked so well the first time on Eve that he figures he'll give it a second shot with us.

So while the Eden gene gets us hankering after something that is not ours to have, the snake encourages us to act on our impatience. He urges us to go out and "get ours." With the hiss of the snake in our ears and a calculated dream in our hearts, we disengage our hand from the palm of the One who is leading us and call back over our shoulder, "I've got this." We may not think we are being disobedient, but just how much more Eve-ish can we get?

When we go in search of Eden, we are saying, "I've had enough of what you want for me, God. I will get my Eden moment. And I will use whatever means I can to get it."

It's not that we don't love Jesus or want him to save us from our sins, but in the deepest corners of our souls dwells a desire that compels us to do what we have to do to get the results we want. The presence of the Eden gene within our souls, that hankering for a perfect life, can unleash all manner of unholiness within us as we try to make our own garden-worthy patch here on earth.

The Eden gene tends to promote two things in us: pride and selfishness. Our pride is that priggish sense of self that reveals we think we are more than we are. We feel we have more resources than we actually do. Clearly, we are delusional at this point. Our selfishness demonstrates that we really don't care what our choices do to our relationships with God and others. We just want what we want. It's not pretty. As long as we are in search of Eden and manipulating others to fall in line with our unrealistic dreams of perfection, it's not going to get any prettier. Get ready to take a look at what the Eden gene yields in the life of the unsuspecting Christ-follower. And you better brace yourself. It looks nothing like Hawaii.

11

I Am Exactly like Eve

When I was in college, I struggled with things like self-esteem, body issues, and clarity as to what life held for me. I was just coming in to my own as an adult and had no real focus as to where I was headed. I was naïve. And looking back, I can see that I was also clueless. Clearly, I was in a perfect position to make some of my life's most important decisions.

I was attending Bible college, and by my junior year I was on my third major. My GPA was dropping due to disinterest and an overactive social life. On top of that, I was thinking that maybe I would become a nun since all forays into male-female relationships had ended in disaster. I wasn't aware of any Protestant nunneries, but I was thinking of starting one. Top that off with my bent toward perfectionism and high expectations and you have a recipe for disaster, or at least a mini nervous breakdown.

During this time of trying to manipulate my life to be what I wanted it to be (changing majors, liking different boys, trying to arrange my future), I experienced a pivotal moment in the campus chapel. I was praying. And by praying, I mean I was telling God what I wanted him to do in my life. And I remember a Scripture passage popping into my head. I looked it up in the Bible. First Corinthians 13:11–12 says, "When I was a child, I spoke and thought and reasoned as a child does. But when I grew up, I put away childish things. Now we see things imperfectly as in a poor mirror, but then we will see everything with perfect clarity. All that I know now is partial and incomplete, but then I will know everything completely, just as God knows me now."

Now, this Scripture passage may seem obscure to you. But I knew exactly what it meant. It was like a God laser beam pinpointing the immature areas of my heart that I needed to yield to God. Sometimes when we pray we really don't want to hear from God; we just like the sound of our own voice. That Scripture passage was like a death knell to me because I wasn't ready to change. God knew I was kidding around with my life. That I was unfocused and irresponsible. That I was fostering questionable relationships. That I was squeaking by by the seat of my spiritual pants, hoping to get in under the radar when it came to confession and repentance. I felt as if he was calling me out: "You say you want to be close to me, but you don't act like it. You don't know what the future holds. You need to put your immature desires behind you and trust me."

I wish I could tell you that at that moment I took a deep breath, exhaled, and shouted a giant yes into the arced ceiling of the chapel. That I threw up my hands in surrender to God, my Creator, the One who shaped my heart and mind. But I would be lying. I remember, with crystal clarity, standing up from that time of prayer with a resolute no resonating in my soul. No, I did not want to yield the most important decisions in my life to a God I could not see and heard only on occasion. No, I did not want to give over the areas of my life that were immature and ill-formed. No, I did not want to stop my pursuit of boys who might not love God but might on the off chance love me. No, I did not want to lose the control I thought I had. *Thought* is the operative word here.

That night was a watershed in my journey with God. It was the first time in all the twenty years of my Christian upbringing that I chose to purposefully walk away from God. The choice was mine. It was a lousy choice. Live and learn, people. And that is what I did. I learned some hard lessons about what happens when you walk away from the God who loves you and knows what is best for you.

That night began my slow descent into hopelessness. When I lost sight of God, I lost sight of who I was. I pulled away from friends who loved me. I chased after boys who didn't. I began to be eaten from the inside out by anxiety and worry. When I became overly anxious, I would get physically ill and would throw up. I found that making myself throw up calmed my nerves, making me feel like I was in control of some small part of my messed-up life. So I continued this pattern. This segued into an eating disorder. I sobbed my way through finals and found myself at semester's end far from God, far from friends, and far from the person I longed to be. It was a lonely, heartbreaking time.

But here is the best part of the story. For the first time in my life, I realized I wasn't good. Not even a little bit. I realized that left to my own plans and devices I would destroy myself and everything good and right in my life. I realized that following my own lead got me nowhere. I was smart enough to realize that I was not the person I longed to be. The girl who had to throw up to make herself feel okay. The girl who had to manipulate boys to feel powerful. The girl who had turned her back on the people who loved her because they didn't agree with her choices. I realized at that key moment that the only person who could redeem the situation I was in and the person I had become was Jesus—the One who forgives and restores. The moment this rang true in my soul, my life moved in a new direction, a direction of forgiveness and grace and mercy. It also led me down a path of counseling and spiritual overhauling as I began to do what I should have done in the chapel. I began to say yes to God.

I know I have been pretty hard on Eve, blaming her for all my shortcomings. My flyaway hair, my overabundance of thigh flesh, and my inability to wave without experiencing a severe underarm jiggle. Clearly, I am not the person I was meant to be in more ways than one. But in all honesty, if I reach back and relive that night in the chapel, when I walked out on God, I can see that I am exactly like her. Wanting more than God is offering. Trying to take control of my life. Wanting to create my own destiny. Walking out on a grace-filled life for a life of my own making. That would be me. And more likely than not, at some point in your life, that would be you. Even today, though I am trying to live my life for the glory of the Creator, I still have to make a choice to yield to the One who is actually in control.

We may not make a conscious decision each day, but our decisions are reflected in the way we live. Do we trust God? Do we? Or are we doing what we can to make our lives look like we want them to? We can say that Jesus is the Lord of our lives, but unless we invite him to weigh in on our daily doings, aren't we lying to ourselves? If we are still trying to manipulate our surroundings to get the results we want, we are being extremely Eve-ish. If we are holding back the immature parts of our hearts for ourselves, unwilling to let God have his way with us, we are walking out on him and his plan for us, just as Eve did.

Now, some of us struggle. We have trouble yielding to anyone, let alone a God we can't see or touch or hear. It seems reasonable that it would be a struggle for us to let him lead us forward. Or does it? Who else has known you like he does? Who else has loved you with such a rich love so long and so true and so all encompassing? Who else will take you any way they can get you and call you their own? Who else has taken your rebukes and your disobedience and your immaturity and said, "I love you still"? Just the Creator. Just the One who has counted the very hairs on your head and knows the length of your days. It is hard not to love him when he went to such extreme lengths to make a way for us to follow him, to know him, and to soak in his presence. What he did on the cross didn't fizzle out on Easter Sunday and wane throughout the centuries. It speaks to the here and now. His love and mercy are still at work in spite of who we are or what we have done.

A love like that cannot be quieted. When we are at our very worst, our most shameful, and our most at odds with him, he keeps on coming with his love. When we demand things of him and walk out on him, when we are our most Eve-ish, when we ruin our good standing and throw away pieces of our hearts to people who do not care, he keeps on coming with his love. When we are broken, wrecked as we never have been before, he keeps on coming with his love. And he is still coming. He can't stop. It is his nature to love us so well.

A love like that can undo a girl. Yes, it can. And it would be smart of you to let it. Let him undo your freakish desire to control everything within a five-mile radius. Let him undo that thing that rises up within you and grasps for perfection. Let him undo those beliefs in your soul that keep you trapped in a pattern of despair. He has your best interests at heart. If you will ask him to, he will lead you in the way everlasting with a sense of joy that comes only when we let him do what he does best. When you feel that nudge, that thing in your gut that is telling you to go forward or to let go or to relax or to wait, that voice that you know is his, you just have to do one thing. With a firm (or shaky will do in a pinch) resolve and an open heart, say, "Yes!" And the best part is, he will take it from there.

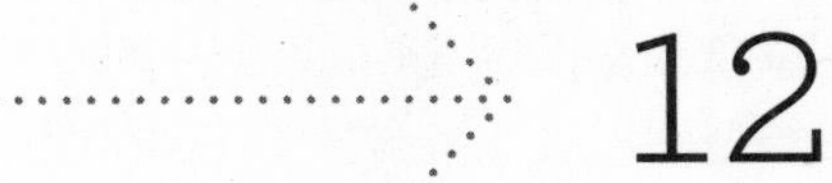

12

I Am a Perfectionist

I have something shocking to say, so if by chance you are reading this standing up, you might want to take a seat. Here it is. Sundays are my least favorite day of the week. I know I have broken the cardinal rule of pastors' wives everywhere (sorry, ladies) and let slip a little-known truth to the general public. Sundays can be difficult. I know I should be more holy since I am a pastor's wife and I come from a long line of Sunday-go-to-meetin' people. It's not that I don't enjoy going to church. But Sundays are the day when chaos rules in my house . . . and sometimes in my soul as well.

This past Sunday is a perfect example. We were nearing the hour when Scott had to load the van and head to church. And I had yet to get materials for the Sunday school class I was teaching. Addison was down for his nap, and Jack and Will were (fingers crossed) playing nicely in Jack's room. I headed out to the store to get some paint and construction paper. When I arrived back home, Scott mentioned casually that our good friends Shane and Marty were coming over to make copies for worship practice. In thirty minutes. I glanced around the house, spotting mounds of laundry on the couch, bills spread out on the table, toys and crumbs littering the floor, and I lost it.

Instead of taking a deep, cleansing breath and rolling with this change of plans, I let loose with a screeching "How could you?" and "Have you seen the house lately?" I frantically began folding clothes and talking rather loudly at my husband. And Scott responded that I was being ridiculous and who cared if the house was clean? Which sent me into another tirade of "Clearly, I care that the house is clean!" which segued into a small pity party of "And I guess I am the only one who does." At one point, Will called out from Jack's room, "Are you and Dad fighting?" to which I answered, "Yes!" and then he followed with, "Are you getting a divorce?" to which I answered, "No!" Jack told me later that maybe Scott and I should fight more so that Will can get used to it and not think we are getting divorced when it happens.

Obviously, I was unraveling. The unpredictability of the day had stripped me bare and laid open my deep-seated need for perfection. If Shane and Marty came to my house when it was in pigsty mode, what would they think of me? It's not that I think people will think I am perfect if my house is clean, but maybe I can fool them into thinking I have it a little more together than I actually do. Or maybe I am just fooling myself. The Eden gene invites us to try to be perfect. Just like Eve was before the fall. It invites us to try to create a world that is like Eden. As if this is a real possibility we can attain.

Perfectionism bleeds into every area of our lives. The work we do. The way we present ourselves. Our attitudes. The way we spend our money. It is open game for the wily ways of the snake because, as we well know, there is no area of our lives that couldn't use a little improvement. The whispers of the snake pull at us, urging us to do more and be more. "If you were prettier, you could have the life you want." Or, "If you could get that job, your career would be set." Or, "If you keep your living room clean, people will respect you more." And we buy into his lies that we are not good enough and our lives aren't good enough either.

There is nothing wrong with wanting to excel in all areas of our lives and bring honor to God with all he has blessed us with, but when we tell ourselves that we have to be perfect to be happy or content, we will never be happy or content. (Drat!) I told my sister Erica the other day, "I have this list in my head of all the things that need to get done before I can consider my day to be a good day. Like finishing the next chapter of the book, having a clean house, spending time with Scott and the kids, and getting to all my emails. And you know what? It never happens all in the same day. So when do I get to have a good day? What am I waiting for?"

Striving for perfection only leads to maintaining a cheap façade that quickly comes crashing down under the weight of reality. Maybe we can attain moments of bliss and glimpses of holiness here and there. But on the whole, life as we know it is messy. And we as people are messy. Our souls are in disarray. We are a hodgepodge of experiences, emotions, future hopes, past hurts, goodness, and sinfulness wrapped up in skin. And when we are caught up in the trap of perfectionism, we are left trying to sort through that mess on our own, piecing together a person and a world that line up with our idea of perfect. Not God's idea, just ours.

So you have a choice. You can keep bending over backward to please yourself and fulfill your ideas of what you think other people expect from you. Or you can give up. Quit striving. Stop trying to perfect yourself and turn to the One who made you. Ask him what he thinks of you. Who he thinks you should be. Is he asking you to be perfect? Is he holding you to standards so high that you cannot possibly reach them? Nope. That would be you. You think you need to be perfect to be lovable in your own eyes or in the eyes of others. In God's eyes, you have always been lovable.

Over coffee one day, I told my friend Lisa how I was struggling. I didn't know how to pull myself together with my relationship with God, with the kids, or with trying to be a good wife. I was failing on so many levels. She said, "Sue, do you think you are Jesus?" I was caught a little off guard by her question.

"No."

"Do you think that somewhere in the near future you might be Jesus?"

I laughed and answered, "No."

"Good," she said. "Then you are off the hook. No one gets to be perfect except Jesus."

Achieving perfection is an impossibility in our lives. The sooner we let ourselves off the hook and realize there is only one Jesus, the better. When God beckons us with his grace, offering us hope for a new life, it is a two-fisted offer. With one hand he offers full forgiveness for all our wrongdoing, past, present, and future, so we can reconnect with him by way of Jesus's righteousness. With the other hand he offers us a chance at a new way of living in which he leads and we follow. He does not forgive our sins and then say, "Give it your best shot, kid. I hope you figure it all out." We don't have to scramble to carve out some semblance of perfection for ourselves. We get to leave all our preconceived notions of what life should look like at the door and ask God to lead the way. To give us a picture of the life he has for us. To nudge our spirits in a path that follows him. If we make knowing him our goal, everything else will fall into place.

Jesus addresses this in the Sermon on the Mount. He is talking to thousands about their fears and worries about the basic necessities of life. (Apparently, those folks were a lot like us.) He tells them not to worry about those things because their Father in heaven already knows their needs. He says in Matthew 6:33, "Seek the Kingdom of God above all else, and live righteously, and he will give you everything you need." He will give you everything you need. Period. Perfectionism is all about our focus. When we try to be perfect, we are focusing all our attention on ourselves, our wants, needs, and desires. When Jesus floods our lives with his grace, he is saying, "Keep looking at me. Keep listening for me. Keep following me. Make me your primary concern, and I will take care of the rest."

Think about that for a second. Do you know what that feeling is that is bursting upon you right now? It is relief. A deep I-couldn't-take-it-one-more-minute relief. Forget about being perfect. He's got you. Let the worry, the anxiety, the feverish cleaning and anxious preening fall to the wayside, and rest in the knowledge that when you put your heavenly Father first, he will meet all your needs and then some. Even when your house is dirty.

13

I Get Discouraged

When I was pregnant with my third son, Addison, I had very distinct ideas about what life would be like after he arrived. I was pretty sure that having three kids was going to be different from having two kids. Obviously, I am brilliant. Like most moms, I was nervous and a little scared, but mostly I was excited. It was going to be a new season for our family. I felt certain that life would assume that rosy glow that accompanies a newborn. A newly painted nursery. A new life. A new start. And all these things were partly true. There was love and fun and a new baby. There was the joy of a new life and the excitement of our family growing. And then there was the reality of what baby number three brought.

What I hadn't counted on when I birthed Addison was the crazy cocktail of sleep depravity and raging hormones that sent my life spinning into a serious bout of postpartum depression. I wasn't ready for the dread that weighed me down as I wrestled with insomnia each night and grew more anxious by the moment, knowing that Addison would be waking to feed soon. I was bowled over by the fact that taking care of two children seemed fairly manageable, while taking care of three had me feeling wild-eyed and frazzled. There was a lot of weeping during those days. Scott was trying to help me and the boys, all the while pouring himself into the upkeep of a new church. The thought of reaching out to anyone at church or otherwise was beyond me. I was in the pit. All my energy was reserved for three small boys who couldn't for the life of them understand why Mommy was so sad all the time.

Each day seemed to get deeper and darker. It was a struggle to get out of bed, to clothe and feed my boys and myself. I had issues with getting a shower. This is often normal for moms of newborns. You would not believe how hard it is to catch five minutes alone with a bar of soap and a razor, but it really is a struggle. I don't know if you know this, but there is no rosy glow when you haven't bathed in three days. I hadn't realized it was possible to wear your hair in a ponytail for an entire year. But it is. I know this because it was my reality. The chasm between the life I expected to be mine and my real life threw me like a wrestler performing a body slam. I was down for the count and at a loss as to what to do.

This was not the life I was hoping for. I was looking for the list. You know, the when-life-is-going-the-way-you-want-it-to list. I wanted to be able to check off all the things that were going right in my life. Healthy baby? Check. Rock-solid marriage? Check. Happy siblings? Check. Prebaby weight miraculously attained upon birth of child? Check. Unfortunately, the healthy baby part was the only thing that could be checked off that list. Maybe I should have made another list. Screaming baby in the night? Check. Super-clingy two-year-old and demanding five-year-old? Check. Distinct lack of spousal communication due to sleepless nights? Check. Belly that feels like Jell-O? Check. I could have checked all those off the list.

I made an appointment with a counselor to see if there was some help for me in this dark place in which I found myself. When I was ushered in to meet with my counselor, Karin, I was a bit nervous, mostly because sharing your innermost thoughts and psychoses with a total stranger can tend to make you feel edgy. I could barely hold it together as she asked me questions about my life, about what filled my days and what made me feel overwhelmed. We chatted for a while, and then she said this: "What, other than being a mom to a five-year-old, a three-year-old, and a four-month-old, a wife to Scott, trying to start a new church, taking care of your family, not having time to write, not sleeping, and surviving in the Bay Area financially, could be worrying you?" We laughed. "I think you are dealing with some very unrealistic expectations," she said. And with those words, something shifted, something hard broke in me, and I began to cry. Then she began to speak words of truth to me, truth about how my life could be good and sweet, even if it didn't look the way I thought it should. Even if there was chaos and sleep depravity and a Jell-O belly. My heart began to heal that day. I think I am healing yet. Expectations are hard to let go of. But when I was holding so tightly to my expectations, I couldn't embrace the joy found in the life I'd been given.

One of the most disconcerting things about the Eden gene is that it makes us think life will go the way we think it should. We are not sure how it is all going to come about in the end, but we feel sure that our days will go according to our plan. A life with no distractions, no hiccups, no disasters, no glitches. Unfortunately, life rarely works out this way, which is heart wrenching for those of us who expect it to. We experience dark days and deep discouragement when things don't go the way we planned.

The Eden gene sets us up for disappointment. If we bank on things going our way all the time, we will find ourselves disillusioned with life. If we believe our good planning and careful organization will yield a smoothly coordinated life, we will be sorely mistaken. Mostly because life is life. It is at best changeable. It is enough to make us throw our hands up in the air and say, "Uncle!" or, "I give!" or whatever it is you say when you feel beaten down by the dailiness of life and the unpredictability of real living.

Proverbs 10:28 says, "The hopes of the godly result in happiness, but the expectations of the wicked are all in vain." Herein lies the key to our dilemma. When Eve walked out of the garden, the ability for life to be what it was supposed to be walked out with her. Life cannot and often will not go the way we think it should. This is a given. But, lo, these many years later, we are still expecting things from life. We are harboring great hopes that our lives will look and feel and smell (a daily shower, please?) like we think they should. As we well know, a hope deferred makes the heart grow sick. Expectations will always leave us wanting. The wise man in Proverbs says they come to nothing.

Now, I am not saying that we are wicked when we expect too much from life, but surely we are misguided. Because life is unpredictable and not always rosy. When we expect things from life or our husband or our children or our office manager and these expectations don't come to fruition, we are often at a loss. We become discouraged and desperate. But it is often mid-moan and in that honest place of despair with our hands thrown up to the sky that it is the best time to remember whose we are and who has us in his palm.

King David says it best in Psalm 42:11: "Why am I discouraged? Why so sad? I will put my hope in God! I will praise him again—my Savior and my God!"

We would do well to follow in David's footsteps, placing our hopes, our expectations in the One who will always come through for us. Life may be unfathomable. Changeable. Cuckoo crazy. But there is one rock-solid, never-changing element in our lives: the Creator. Our well-being and expectations can't be rooted in the hopes that our day will turn out the way we want it to. Our well-being needs to be anchored in the hope that God will be with us in the ins and outs of our days. Our souls need to be moored to the fact that God is who he says he is and will do what he promised, working all things together for the good of those who love him. We have to make a conscious shift from thinking that our lives must go the way we want them to, to thinking that God will be who he has always been in our lives. Faithful. Protective. Loving. Omnipotent.

The hopes of the godly don't result in happiness because everything always goes the way it should for the godly. The godly have serious troubles and issues too. Rather, the hopes of the godly result in happiness because they know that when they place their lives in the care of the One who loves them best, they are giving him the opportunity to come through for them. To save them. To deliver them. To hold them close. To encourage their spirits and wipe their tears. To guide them and to put a new song in their hearts. And to give them a peace that comes only when his Spirit is dwelling in them. Even when they have worn their hair in a ponytail for forty-one consecutive days. And that is something you can bank on.

14

I Have Control Issues . . . Big Ones

If I had cable television, I would never get a lick of work done. I would be hunkered down watching home design shows from nine to five. Those shows make me giddy. I especially love the organizing shows when the organizer goes in and declutters a home. Sometimes just seeing the clutter makes me feel claustrophobic, and I have to start cleaning out a closet of my own. But, lo and behold, when the designer begins to cleanse and purge, I have to keep myself from cheering out loud, because who would not want to be free of all that junk? Now the homeowners will have a bedroom free from trampolines and Victorian dolls and will be able to see their bed again. A victory has been won! They are free from the clutter and despair, and now they have matching bins for all their children's toys. Is there anything more joyful than matching bins? Is there? I don't think so.

I used to have a business where I organized people's houses. I would go in and file and purge and put everything in matching bins. (I love you, matching bins!) When a job was finished, I would feel ecstatic. Everything was in order. But you should also know that just because I organized other people's homes does not mean that my house is organized. I am full of grand plans and dreams, but ever since the children arrived, keeping our house organized has been like trying to hold back the tide. I cannot tell you what that does to my insides. Even now I am thinking I should quit writing and go sort through some toys because most nights I have to perform ninja-like gymnastics to get from the boys' door to their beds to tuck them in. Their closets make me want to keel over from despair. And all the various papers that have made it into the house in the last three weeks are stacked on my dryer, hidden under a blue-and-white-striped towel. I put the towel there so I won't have to look at them until I can find time to file them properly. Clearly, I have issues. Control issues. Welcome to the untidy world I live in. I blame Eve.

When Eve decided to take her own destiny in hand, she probably didn't realize she would be dealing with the fallout of that decision for the rest of her life. When there is fallout in our lives, we have two choices. We can turn to the One who has all the resources in the world to deal with the fallout, or we can go it alone. The snake is keen on us going it alone. He wants us isolated from the One who knows us inside and out. He wants us to fail miserably. If he can get us to go it alone, if he can urge us to try to heal our own hurts and bind up our own wounds using less than stellar methods, he will triumph. He likes to say things like, "You've got this. If you get the right flow chart going, you can organize your life." Or, "If you can cut out all fat in your diet for seven months, you can rule the world." Or, "If you do this exercise regimen, your life's problems will melt away."

His suggestions seem so wise and prudent. Organization, a good diet, and exercise are all necessities in life. All the snake has to do is get us thinking this way and let the Eden gene do the rest. The Eden gene rises up within us and convinces us that if we run our lives a certain way we will be free and will be able to manage all our problems. It makes us think we are in control and can achieve the lives we want on our own. As if an organizational system or a new diet or three hours of nonstop cardio are enough to change the patterns of our hearts. As if micromanaging calories can release the hurt that dwells in our souls.

That is the craziness of the Eden gene. We feel we have the ability to put our world right using whatever methods seem right to us. Instead of using alcohol or drugs or food to escape from our troubles, those of us with control issues use positive things like fitness regimes and filing systems to make ourselves feel safe. We soothe ourselves by pouring ourselves into our work or mapping out our lives with goals to manage the chaos. We try to quell the disquiet in our lives by managing the minutiae down to the last *t* that needs crossing.

Now, you may not think you have an inner control freak, but if you tend to have a nervous breakdown over someone folding a towel in half rather than doing a nice trifold, you do. If you have micromanaged your calendar, charting everything from your daily teeth flossing to your garbage pickups, you do. If your spice rack is alphabetized, you do. If you have ever limited your diet to tofu and kale, you do. If you have ever become overcome with joy at the sight of a spreadsheet, you do. Welcome to control freaks anonymous. I'll be the first to introduce myself. Hi, my name is Susanna, and I am a control freak.

Usually, those of us with control issues are high-minded. We are working for the common good. We're not escaping reality with drugs and Ho Hos here. We are confronting real life head-on. Shaping it into what it needs to look like. We are embracing positive things like good health and stability and clean cupboards, for goodness' sake. People may be a bit put off by our neurotic tendencies, but we are striving for order and clarity and matching bins. Whatever your glitch is, whether it's closet organizers or to-do lists, I have a sorry bit of news for you. In the long run, it's not going to cut it. The snake lied. Matching bins are not going to order your life. And that Eden gene vibe you've got going on, the one that tells you if you just stick to eating tofu and kale that the planets will come into alignment and all will be right with the world, that's not working either.

Usually, the thing we use to control our environment (e.g., our eating regimen, our organizational creed, our fanatical towel folding) ends up controlling us. We become so hemmed in by the methods we are using that we can't get free of them. The very thing we are shaping our lives with can create chaos in our souls. Our organizing can become obsessive. Our eating regimen can plummet into a disorder. Our attempts to rule our lives with systems can keep us from living the life of freedom we were created for.

Here is the thing. There is only one person who knows how to right the wrongs in our world. And he doesn't use bins or filing systems or kale. (As far as I know, he has nothing against any of these things, but the life we are longing for does not lie with them.) We tend to forget that the Creator of the garden fashioned our lives. He needs freedom to shape and mold our lives into the design he planned for us. He does not want us bound up in methods and rituals, trying to make sense of the lives he gave us. He would like to make sense of them for us. Proverbs 3:5–6 says, "Trust in the LORD with all your heart; do not depend on your own understanding. Seek his will in all you do, and he will direct your paths."

Trusting God with the minutiae of our lives can be the act that begins to set us free. God didn't design us to be control freaks. Control freaks are so, you know, controlling. They are usually tense, worried, and hopped up on caffeine . . . or maybe that is just me. God has more for us in mind. It is not that God doesn't love order and planning. Take a look at the solar system. Pretty well-ordered and planned, isn't it? It is the fact that we think we can out-plan and out-order God. We think we are in charge, when in fact we are his kids and he is in charge. Spending time with him, getting to know what he thinks about things, lets us be kids who know that he has everything under control, kids who know that our heavenly Father has the resources of the world at his fingertips and can take care of anything that comes up, kids who know that sometimes our Father thinks outside the box, and although his will may not look like we think it should, in it we will find life and truth and freedom.

God's will for us often defies logic and analysis. It can sound crazy and whacked out. Just ask Abraham, Noah, or Moses. But Abraham, Noah, and Moses knew something else too. God always keeps his promises. Always. We can let go of those systems and habits and controlling tendencies that keep us enslaved and realize that we can be set free when we trust him. He says that if we trust him with our hearts he will make a way for us in this life. He means it. Our Father never lies. And that, my friends, is way better than matching bins.

15

I Don't Like Waiting

Due to a recent back injury, I have spent a good amount of time lying on my couch. I have always liked my couch, but lately we have grown remarkably close. I have also developed a deep affection for my laptop. I can lie on my back, prop it up on my legs, and still be connected to the outside world, all the while remaining on my couch. This is a good thing, since I found out my back could be hurting for a long time. Just typing that out makes me sad inside. But being best friends with my laptop and all, I have found I can order a wide array of things online while keeping my back completely flat. This makes Scott sad inside. He knows I am in a weakened condition and could spend irrationally.

But he shouldn't worry. Mostly I am ordering birthday presents and books. Reading is a couch-friendly activity. The only problem with ordering books on the internet is that I have to wait for them. The stores increase the suspense by sending me tracking numbers so I can watch as my books make their way to my mailbox. I track them vigilantly. I sent my dad a book for his birthday. When he said it hadn't arrived by the estimated shipping date, I immediately got online and checked. I called him back and made him check the perimeter of his house because the status read "delivered." I think I was more excited than he was when he found it. Last night I yelled out, "Granny's candy is in Kentucky!" No one had any idea what I was talking about. Scott's grandma had recently broken her hip and was in the hospital, so I had ordered her some See's candy. People with broken hips need all the chocolate they can get. I can hardly wait for my books to arrive or for my presents to get where I've sent them. I'm no good at waiting. I'm like our five-year-old, Addison, who says, "It's taking tooooooooo long!" Waiting offends us. It's not our gifting.

Waiting wasn't Eve's gifting either. She was chomping at the bit once the snake told her how fantastic that fruit was. It would have stood us all in good stead if Eve had said, "Let me think about this." Even better, if she had turned and said, "Thanks, but no thanks!" to that lousy snake. If only she had waited a bit before making such a rash decision or had run a few laps around the garden before taking matters into her own hands. Maybe the outcome could have been different.

Eve passed that tendency for impatience down to us as a part of the Eden gene. Waiting seems so wasteful and unproductive. I prefer not to wait. I want to get what I want . . . now. Eve and I are not alone in our struggle. Everyone hates waiting. Especially for something God has promised us. Sarah hated waiting, that's for sure (Gen. 15–16). Sarah waited and waited and waited for God to give her a son. All she wanted was a baby to hold in her arms. Someone to carry on the family name. A son that she and Abraham could be proud of. And God promised them that they would not be disappointed. There would be a son, and their descendants would be as numerous as the stars in the sky. God said there would be kings in their family line. Kings! He said that, and then they waited. And waited. Sarah waited for years.

Eventually, Sarah became disillusioned with the waiting. She began to doubt God's promise. She decided to take matters into her own hands. This is never good. It is understandable but not good. She decided she would get God's promise one way or another. You can bet the snake was in on this one, egging her on and whispering lies in her ear. Sarah had Abraham sleep with her servant, Hagar. (Let us just note that having your husband sleep with someone else is never a good idea.) When Hagar became pregnant, Sarah felt even worse than before. Hagar taunted her, and Sarah lost her cool and treated her harshly. It went from bad to worse. Sarah was a wreck, Hagar was distraught, and Abraham was caught in the middle. All because Sarah couldn't wait.

The Eden gene invites us to think that our timetable is the right timetable, that we should have whatever we want whenever we want it, and that we know better than God. We feel that waiting is a stall out. How can there be any growth or movement when we are on hold? We could be doing things, setting the world on fire with our goals and our dreams, if only God would make his move. If only he would give us what he promised us. If only.

We become impatient when we don't understand how God works. We don't understand his timing. We don't understand his plans. Eve didn't. Sarah didn't. We don't. But here is the thing. God knows things we don't know. He knows exactly the right time and the right place that things should occur.

He is the Creator of the universe, after all. He reminds the Israelites of this in Isaiah 55:8–11:

> "My thoughts are completely different from yours," says the Lord. "And my ways are far beyond anything you could imagine. For just as the heavens are higher than the earth, so are my ways higher than your ways and my thoughts higher than your thoughts.
>
> "The rain and snow come down from the heavens and stay on the ground to water the earth. They cause the grain to grow, producing seed for the farmer and bread for the hungry. It is the same with my word. I send it out, and it always produces fruit. It will accomplish all I want it to, and it will prosper everywhere I send it."

God is not bragging. He doesn't have to. He is great. Immovable. Immutable. Unchangeable. Omnipotent. Omniscient. Omnipresent. And don't forget that he is on our side. He really wants to see us get what he has promised us. He is not just messing with us. He has a plan. This is why the Bible urges us time after time to "wait on the Lord." Wait. Listen. And then wait some more. It makes a difference. Not only does waiting give us some time to clear our heads and get our priorities straight, but it also helps us recognize God for who he is. The inventor of time. Don't you think that if God made time and works through time that he will do what he needs to do in exactly the right time? There are so many promises to be had, so many victories to be won, so many gifts to behold if we choose to ignore the clamoring of the Eden gene and our own agenda and wait on what God has for us.

Maybe you have been waiting for years on end like Sarah. The snake would like you to think that God's plan for you has petered out. That he can't possibly be interested in your heartache or keep his promise to you. But don't give him the time of day. God has not forgotten you. God promised Sarah a baby when she was sixty-six. She had Isaac when she was ninety. That is a twenty-four-year gestational period, people. No wonder Sarah lost sight of God's promise. If you are waiting and you think you cannot wait one more minute for God to come through, he knows that too. If you think you cannot go on waiting because he is already too late, just remember what he told his people in the Old Testament:

> O Israel, how can you say the Lord does not see your troubles? How can you say God refuses to hear your case? Have you never heard or understood? Don't you know that the Lord is the everlasting God, the Creator of all the earth? He never grows faint or weary. No one can measure the depths of his understanding. He gives power to those who are tired and worn out; he offers strength to the weak. Even youths will become exhausted, and young men will give up. But those who wait on the Lord will find new strength. They will fly high on wings like eagles. They will run and not grow weary. They will walk and not faint. (Isa. 40:27–31)

In some translations, this passage says, "Those who *hope* in the Lord will renew their strength." Apparently, hoping and waiting are interchangeable. This is not waiting in the sense that we will never see a solution or an answer to our problems. This is waiting in the sense that the One we are waiting on has every intention of bringing about an answer in his timing, which, although it is not our timing, is perfect and providential. We can place all our hopes in God, knowing that when we are on our last leg, thinking we cannot hold on a minute more, he sees our predicament and he is with us—hemming us in before and behind, lifting us up on eagles' wings, giving us new strength for the days that lie ahead.

He sees you. He hears you. He knows all about you. He knows what has you stuck. He knows what your hopes and dreams are, and if you are willing to wait on him, he will hold you up. He will come through for you. He will breathe life into your weary body and give you wings to fly. The waiting won't last forever. He promises. Keep holding on, and he will birth something in you that you never thought possible. Just ask Sarah. She knows.

16

I Can Get a Little Bitter

I've struggled on and off with bouts of depression since having postpartum depression with my third son. As the years pass, the struggles seem to be less frequent, but if I have to be honest, I would really like a depression-free life. I was pretty even-keeled before, at least that's what Scott tells me, and I believe him because he has a better memory than I do. Sometimes it ticks me off when I think about it. Why do I struggle with depression? Why couldn't I be the way I was before? I don't want depression to be a part of my story. The depressed pastor's wife. The angst-ridden author. The manic mother. Those things sound terrible! And believe me, they feel even more terrible than they sound. While I feel that each day I gain a little more equilibrium and am able to stand a little firmer in the belief that God is healing me, there are still moments that pull me down, reminding me how tenuous my joy and emotional stability can be.

When I am depressed, the depression sucks all hope out of my day. The air seems thinner, and it's harder to breathe.

The smallest obligation can crush me. The teensiest conflict can overwhelm me. These days are all about survival. The best way I can describe it is that it feels like I am mired in sludge, and just making it to the end of the day takes all my strength—physically, emotionally, and spiritually. Depression is lousy. I'm not going to lie. When I have those dark days, I think to myself, "This is definitely not the person I want to be. I didn't choose this! Why did my body and mind turn on me like this?" And then I find myself a little bitter. Angry for what life has brought. And maybe a bit desperate. Will it ever be better?

Sometimes I wonder what Eve felt like after she got booted out of the garden. I wonder if she was depressed, embittered, disillusioned. I wonder if she ever got her joy back. It's always tough when we have to walk out the consequences of our sin. It's even tougher when bad things happen that have nothing to do with our choices. Events like that can take us to a hopeless place. The tragedies of life, chronic illnesses, financial disasters, even the mundane and boring things that shape our days can get us focusing on the negative things in our lives.

This is the Eden gene at work again. Just as it encourages our unrealistic expectations of the future, it also encourages us to harbor memories of the past. Either we cling to the glory days, reliving those seasons of life when things were coming together beautifully and we felt blessed, or we ruminate about all the terrible things that have happened in the past and become certain that the future holds only more pain for us.

Life can be extremely painful at times. A failed marriage. A loss of a job. Disillusionment with the church. A collapse of a friendship. A death in the family. When we are dealt these hard blows, we can't help looking back to our past, saying, "I wish life was like that again. I want to go back to that place." Or if life just keeps dealing us one blow after the next, we say, "Now life is always going to be horrible. It will never get any better than this." As long as the Eden gene has us living in the past, the snake wins. Because if we are stuck in the past, we lose out on our future. We get lost in hopelessness and stuck in bitterness. We get mired in a life pattern in which we're mad either because our life was so much better before or because life has always been awful and we can't see how it can turn around.

Naomi is a perfect example of this. If you have read the book of Ruth in the Old Testament, you know who I am talking about. Naomi and her husband, Elimelech, were from Bethlehem. They left Israel during a famine and settled in Moab. Their sons, Mahlon and Kilion, married two Moabite women, Ruth and Orpah. While they were in Moab, Elimelech died, leaving Naomi to be cared for by her sons. When her sons both died, Naomi was completely devastated, which is understandable. Surely, this is too much tragedy for one woman to bear. Naomi thought so. She was at a loss as to what to do. This wasn't how her life was supposed to go. She tried to leave her daughters-in-law in Moab, urging them to remarry, but Ruth wouldn't hear of it. The only thing Naomi knew to do was to go back to Bethlehem. When Ruth refused to leave her, Naomi took her back to Bethlehem, causing quite a stir.

> So the two of them continued on their journey. When they came to Bethlehem, the entire town was stirred by their arrival. "Is it really Naomi?" the women asked.
>
> "Don't call me Naomi," she told them. "Instead, call me Mara, for the Almighty has made life very bitter for me. I

> went away full, but the LORD has brought me home empty. Why should you call me Naomi when the LORD has caused me to suffer and the Almighty has sent such tragedy?" (Ruth 1:19–21)

I'm not a psychologist, but I am pretty sure Naomi was depressed. And ticked off. She contemplated a drastic name change. Naomi means "pleasant," whereas Mara means "bitter." Naomi was headed down the path to becoming a glass-half-empty kind of lady. Or a my-glass-is-shattered-and-I'll-never-drink-again kind of lady. She could not get past all she had lost in Moab. Love and family and stability were gone. She believed that her tragedy defined her and that there was only more of the same to be had in the future. She was completely stuck. Exhausted. Disappointed in life. "Through," as my friend Rodney would say.

I have known a lot of people like Naomi. I may or may not be like her on occasion. Okay, I am like her on occasion, but my husband, Scott, is the opposite. He is an optimist. He is the polar opposite of Naomi. He believes that what God has for us in the future will completely outdo the past. He is a visionary. (Church planters usually are.) Scott is always dwelling on a positive thought. He encourages people and has a fantastic sense of humor. Scott sees the good in the midst of any hardship. I know, it's sickening. Sometimes living with such goodness can be a trial to one's soul, especially if one tends to be more negative. Not that I am. Okay, I am. And I really want Jesus to change that about me, but maybe if Scott could be a little less cheery, it would make things easier.

When I first met Scott, his excitement about life was one of the things I couldn't get enough of. He was excited about being a youth pastor. He loved hanging out and laughing with his friends. He was leading a rap ministry that went into schools and prisons to share God's love. (Yep, I married a rapper . . . holla!) Now, you may think that Scott is so cheery because he had a fantastic childhood, that he has never experienced tragedy or faced hardship. But that would be untrue. The first rap I ever heard him perform was the story of his testimony. It had a sweet hook that would keep you singing for days. ("I don't need no blunt. I don't need no forty. I just need the Lord and nothin' else. No, nothing more, G." Catchy, right?) But it was the story told between the hook that caught my attention.

The song starts out telling how Scott and his sister, Cheri, were brought up in an alcoholic's home. Scott's mom, Sandy, loved the Lord, but his dad wanted nothing to do with Jesus. When he got drunk, he and Sandy would fight. Scott and Cheri would cry in bed at night, scared for their mom. While Scott's dad loved Scott and Cheri like crazy, he couldn't seem to hold his marriage together. When it began to unravel, he picked up Scott and Cheri from school one day and kidnapped them for a year and a half. For a year and a half they didn't get to see their mom. They ping-ponged across the country and landed in Alabama. After Scott's dad and mom worked out a divorce over the phone, they went back to California to live for good. Scott ends the song by saying, "But through all of that I came to see that I can never live my life without my G-o-d."

I remember thinking after hearing that song, "How can he look at life the way he does when his childhood was so difficult? How does a ten-year-old kid come through something like that unscathed?" And when I got to know Cheri and Sandy, wouldn't you know it, they were as cheery as Scott.

Cheri could be the poster child for "happy." No matter what life throws her way, she believes the best is yet to come. When I asked Scott's mom how she made it through a year and a half without seeing her kids (a thing that would flatten me for sure), she said, "I always knew they would come back. I had peace. The Lord promised me he would bring them back." Scott's family is on to something. They know there is always more to the story. Hope is not lost. If you can just hang on, if you can lean on the Lord and hope in him, the story can get good. Really good.

When we get stuck in our past, in the goodness or the rottenness of it, we are so focused on the previous chapter of our lives that we forget there is still more story to be told. We forget who is writing our story. We forget the author and finisher of our faith. We forget about the One who knows every plot twist in our personal history. And we forget the most important thing of all. He always gets the last word. Our bitterness can blind us to the fact that as long as we are still breathing, however difficult life may be, the story is not over. Not for Naomi. Not for Ruth. Not for Scott. Not for Cheri. Not for Sandy. Not for me. Not for you.

No, granted, sometimes we can't see how in the world God can make the leap from one chapter to the next, but that is not our job. We don't have to understand how he can bring order from our chaos. We just have to believe that he can. We have to remember that he can move mountains and cast out demons and heal hurts and redeem broken things. God is innately creative and resourceful. We don't know how he can take our hardships, our hurts, and our tragedies and work them into our story line in a positive way, but the apostle Paul reminds us that he can. Romans 8:28 says, "And we know that God causes everything to work together for the good of those who love God and are called according to his purpose for them."

God can and he does. Just ask Naomi. When Ruth married Boaz, Naomi got the best son-in-law a woman could ask for. She was provided for and loved until the end of her days. God is still working on our behalf today. Just ask Sandy. God brought her Dave, my father-in-law, who loves her like crazy. And all these years later, both her kids are following hard after Jesus and live within fifteen minutes of her house. Just ask me. There is this man named Scott. Even on my darkest days, he is there with a word of hope, a hug, and sometimes, if I am lucky, a piece of chocolate. We can't forget. The Author is still at work. Writing our stories, shaping our lives, reworking the rough spots, editing our dreams, bringing hope and light and redemption. If we can take our eyes off the past and place our hopes and dreams in him, he will write the stories of our lives in such a way that we will never be the same. Can I get an amen?

17

I Am a Little Self-Centered

One day when my youngest son, Addison, was around eighteen months old, I had an odd moment of quiet in my house. When you have an eighteen-month-old around, this is never good. I began to search for him and found him in my closet surrounded by pieces of red and green tinfoil, with chocolate smeared all over his face. He had found a hidden stash of candy from Christmas. This was in April, by the way, so the candy was not at its freshest. But Addison didn't seem to mind. I asked him point-blank, "Addison, have you been eating chocolate?"

He said, "No." He said this with chocolate-covered lips.

So I looked at him and said, "Addison, don't lie to Mommy. Tell me the truth. Have you been eating chocolate?"

He looked at me with a look that said, "You're good, lady! How could you tell?" and said, "Yeth," in his sweet toddler lisp. He had to come clean. I had hard evidence against him.

Our house rule is that you have to ask before you can eat candy. Maybe you are thinking, "He was so little. He didn't know." But I must point out that the child hid in a closet and did not make a peep. He went off the grid. Now, I understand the powers that chocolate wields and their ability to break a person down. I can hardly blame him. In fact, I was more than a little ticked off that Addison found that secret stash of candy and didn't share. But here is the thing. There was no way in the world my toddler was going to find the hidden treasure of candy and divvy it up with the family. He was keeping that deliciousness all to himself. From infancy to adulthood, we are selfish. We think the universe revolves around us, and we don't change as we get older. We just get better at hiding it. When we're adults, we know to get rid of the wrappers and clean off our faces before someone finds out and wants in on our chocolate. We get craftier and sneakier and more manipulative. We are out to get what we want no matter what the cost. You know, just like Eve. Selfish behavior is the telltale sign of the Eden gene.

Despite all my obvious irritation at Eve, I really do have a fondness for her. She was anxious to get everything out of life that she could. She liked to eat. And more than anything, she wanted to make sure that the most important person in the world was taken care of. Herself. Clearly, we are related. She was completely egocentric. She was thinking about herself when she ate the apple. Not God. Not Adam. Not the snake. Just herself. And I relate to that in every way. I think about myself constantly. Even when I'm not trying to think about myself, I do. You'd think I would get bored. But I find the subject riveting. It seems I am not alone in this. Whereas some of us may vary in our degrees of perfectionism or control issues, all of humanity bears the mark of self-centeredness.

The Bible tells story after story of people who followed in Eve's selfish footsteps, fighting for what they wanted and stepping on people to get their own way. The story of Jacob's family line alone is enough to keep you reeling. The trickery and conniving that went on in that family is mind-numbing. Isaac and Rebekah had twin boys, Esau and Jacob. Isaac loved Esau more, and Rebekah loved Jacob more. (Picking favorites never bodes well in the familial setting.) Rebekah wanted to make sure that Jacob got his fair share and set about making it come to pass. Jacob tricked Esau into giving him his birthright. Rebekah tricked Isaac into thinking Jacob was Esau so he would get his father's blessing. Jacob stole Esau's blessing. Jacob fled to his uncle Laban's house because Esau wanted to kill him. Jacob fell in love with Laban's daughter, Rachel, and agreed to work for Laban for seven years in exchange for her hand in marriage. Laban lied to Jacob, tricking him into marrying his older daughter, Leah, when Jacob thought he was marrying Rachel. Laban forced Jacob to work another seven years in exchange for Rachel. Jacob got tired of Laban cheating him and took off in the night with his wives. Rachel stole her father's household idols in the process. Laban tracked them down and demanded the idols. Rachel lied about having the idols. And on and on and on it goes. In a word? Selfish. In two words? Cuckoo crazy.

Jacob, Laban, and Rachel all had one person in mind as they laid out their plans and hatched their schemes. Themselves. Egocentric thinking is humanity's default mode. The controlling? The perfectionism? The striving? The ambitiousness? They all spring from the well of self-centeredness within us. Left to our own devices, we quickly give in to self and the whims and wants that seem to benefit us the most. Not one of us is different from Eve or Jacob or Laban or Rachel . . . or Addison, for that matter. Well, there is one.

One man lived his entire life for the benefit of others. Jesus. Clearly, if we think about it, we can see that he lived his life to benefit . . . us. His life, his words, his character are so opposite from ours. I suppose it is because instead of centering his life around himself and his desires, he centered it around God, his Father. He wasn't self-centered. He was selfless. Paul reminds the Christians in Philippi about this, saying, "Don't be selfish; don't live to make a good impression on others. Be humble, thinking of others as better than yourself. Don't think only about your own affairs, but be interested in others, too" (2:3–4). (Clearly, the Philippians struggled with some of the same issues you and I do.) The passage goes on to say:

> Your attitude should be the same that Christ Jesus had. Though he was God, he did not demand and cling to his rights as God. He made himself nothing; he took the humble position of a slave and appeared in human form. And in human form he obediently humbled himself even further by dying a criminal's death on a cross. Because of this, God raised him up to the heights of heaven and gave him a name that is above every other name, so that at the name of Jesus every knee will bow, in heaven and on earth and under the earth, and every tongue will confess that Jesus Christ is Lord, to the glory of God the Father. (Phil. 2:5–11)

What Jesus did on the cross is the antithesis of what Eve did in the garden. Eve walked away from God. Jesus submitted his entire being to him. Eve turned her back on the destiny God had for her. Jesus walked it out, moment by moment, until he drew his last breath. Eve listened to the snake. Jesus silenced him. Eve thought of no one but herself. Jesus thought of every man, woman, and child since the inception of the world instead of himself. Instead of taking what he could, he gave all he had. Instead of conniving and manipulating to get things his way, he became a servant, a slave, humbling himself, pouring himself out so that we could have a chance to know the Creator again. Without him, all hope is lost. With him, all hope is gained.

We are looking for the keys to the kingdom. We want to live out our dreams. We want security and wealth. We want perfection and control. We want Eden. But we are missing the point. What we want and what we truly need are two different things. We don't need a place or a set of perfect circumstances. We don't need a chain of events that fix everything. We need a person. A person who loved us more than his own life. A person who was willing to let go of all his rights. A person who was raised from the dead and who shattered hell and the hold its keeper had on the world. Jesus. The name at which every knee should bow and every tongue confess that he is Lord.

This is our chance. Our moment, if you will. We can keep on striving and struggling, trying to find that perfect place in life where everything looks and feels like it is going our way. We can keep grasping for a life we will never have, or we can let go—let go of the mounting pressure that presses in as we fail ourselves over and over, let go of the thoughts that drive us to keep trying to control others, let go of the fallacy that we can reach heaven here on earth—and with both hands grab on to the One who can set us free. He sets us free from the desires that keep us trapped, from the gnawing hunger that is in us to be perfect in every way, from the drive that keeps us focusing on ourselves. He sets us free to follow the destiny the Creator has for us. Whom the Son has set free is free indeed. There is just one question for you. Are you ready to be free?

18

I Am a Rule Follower

When I was a kid, my mom said I was a curious child. That is a mother's love speaking, because I was unruly and wild. I knew all the rules. I just didn't like following them. I brought frogs in the house. I stole candy. I scraped my sister's face with a Mickey Mouse night-light when she wouldn't give it to me. I snuck out of Sunday school and ran down the middle aisle of the adult service while my dad was preaching, so I could be with him on the platform. One Sunday night communion service, during a holy moment, my mom got up to take me out into the lobby to discipline me for the third time, and I yelled out into the worshipful atmosphere, "Oh no! Not again!" I think I made my mom want to pull all of her hair out. Because I was curious.

But somewhere in between childhood and adulthood, I leveled out, and risk taking lost its pull for me. I made it through junior high and high school without a serious rebellion. The Bible college I went to had strict lifestyle guidelines. The greatest break I made with the rules was smoking a corncob pipe with my friend Leslie on the beach. I immediately felt so guilty that I made a full confession at the student life office. (I was laughed out of the office.) Instead of pushing boundaries, I stuck to them. I had a great fear of being caught and getting punished, so I did what I was told.

This rule following has leaked into most areas of my adult life. I go into the less-than-fifteen-items line at the store only after I have counted the items in my cart. I never drive in the carpool lane by myself. I send in my taxes on time. I don't cuss. I'm a by-the-book kind of girl. Especially when it comes to God. I do my best to stay on the straight and narrow. I set up lots of rules for myself to remind me to be a good disciple. I try to set aside time with God each day (I think calling on him while paying the bills counts). I go to church every week (this is a given since skipping out can cause marital strife). I dress modestly (e.g., no tube tops, short shorts, or half shirts—this is also for the protection of the general public. I don't want them to claw out their eyes in my presence.). There is definitely no corncob pipe smoking. I love rules because rules make me feel safe. They are black-and-white, and I know where I stand with the rules. I also like rules because when I know where *you* stand with the rules, it makes it easier for me to judge you. (Did I just write that out loud? It's true. I am a judger. Most people who like rules are.)

Perfectionist control freaks are usually a bit obsessive about the rules and like to tattle. If I see someone in a tube top and tiny shorts, I am immediately worried that their tube top may fall down at any moment. The law of gravity counts as a rule. I also tend to look at them with disdain because they are showing too much thigh, which goes against my modest dress rule. I want to tattle to God and point out that my shorts come to my knees and I am wearing proper foundational garments. I hope God will speak a word to Daisy Duke over there about appropriate dressing. (I'm more offended if they look good in their tube top and shorts because then I feel they are being rewarded for breaking the rules.) Most days are a downward spiral for me with my rules. I usually end up disappointed in myself for not being able to meet my own standards, and I am equally disappointed with everyone around me for being so full of sin. I may or may not be a hypocrite. Okay, I am.

Eve left us in a rules quandary. She had one rule to follow, and she broke it. We've been trying to toe the line ever since. We think we can be good if we try hard enough, but it is such a struggle with the sin nature and all. The Eden gene promotes the thought that if we follow all the rules we can earn our way into God's good graces. We think that if we are good, God will love us more. The snake loves this thinking because it is delusional in two ways: (1) we think we have the ability to tally up goody points to get Jesus to love us, and (2) we think we have the right to judge others who don't follow the rules. We get two sins for the price of one: pride and judging others. And, of course, we are missing the point completely. God is not impressed when we follow the rules. The way we act needs to flow out of our love for him, not out of our desire to appear holy. We see this clearly when Jesus comes in contact with the Pharisees, the religious leaders of his day. He doesn't cut them a whole lot of slack with their rules.

The Pharisees loved rules. They had rules for everything from Sabbath behavior to eating requirements to personal cleanliness, and if you didn't follow their rules, well, then you obviously didn't love God. Actually, they loved their rules more than they loved God. Jesus may have had most of his fun on earth breaking their rules. The Pharisees had hissy fits left and right because of how Jesus acted. He healed people on the Sabbath. He ate with tax collectors and partiers. He cared about riffraff and played with children. He caused a scandal when a woman of ill repute washed his feet with her tears and dried them with her hair.

Jesus didn't pull any punches with them either. He called the Pharisees names like hypocrites and blind men and snakes, which is interesting in light of what we know about our enemy the snake. Jesus said outright in Matthew 23:27–28, "How terrible it will be for you teachers of religious law and you Pharisees. Hypocrites! You are like whitewashed tombs—beautiful on the outside but filled on the inside with dead people's bones and all sorts of impurity. You try to look like upright people outwardly, but inside your hearts are filled with hypocrisy and lawlessness."

When it came to rule lovers, Jesus didn't mess around. Nope. He said they cleaned up nice on the outside but inside, not so much. When the Pharisees acted holier than thou, they weren't pleasing God. They were just lying to themselves. And when it got to be too much, when Jesus's mercy and love and miracles showed them up for who they really were—fakers—they killed him. When I read about them, I think, "Ooh, they are horrible! I hope God gets them good." And then I think, "I'm one of them!" Because I like pretending I am good. I have trouble looking past people's sins and caring for them in spite of themselves. It is easier for me to judge than to love. And it is easier to follow my own rules than to listen for God's direction in my life. Just like them, when I think I can please God on my own merit, when I play the part of the Pharisee, I kill any chance of Jesus working in my life.

The apostle Paul understood this. Probably because he was a Pharisee's Pharisee named Saul before he met Jesus. Saul was so committed to keeping the rules of the Jewish faith that he hunted down Christians and killed them for breaking the Mosaic law. Meeting Jesus on the road to Damascus changed everything. Bowed and blinded in the presence of Jesus, Saul saw himself for who he was. A sinner. He began to understand that life was not about following rules. Life was about loving the One who offered a life full of grace and forgiveness. Coming in contact with Jesus so radically changed Saul that he changed his name to Paul. His life's mission shifted from punishing those who broke the rules to following the Messiah and telling others about him. Everything he cherished before as a Pharisee was junk to him now. Paul said, "Yes, everything else is worthless when compared with the priceless gain of knowing Christ Jesus my Lord. I have discarded everything else, counting it all as garbage, so that I may have Christ and become one with him. I no longer count on my own goodness or my ability to obey God's law, but I trust Christ to save me. For God's way of making us right with himself depends on faith" (Phil. 3:8–9).

Paul came away from his encounter with Jesus a changed man. We are no different. Jesus's holiness and his love for us are our undoing. Most of us just become mean and judgmental when we try to be good. Jesus's holiness allowed him to pay the price for our wrongs and shows us who we are. Sinners. In the presence of his rightness, we see all our wrongness. But in the presence of his rightness, we don't find judgment; we find forgiveness. And hope. He does not call us to a life of good behavior. He calls us to a life filled with him. When we follow Jesus, it is not about rules and tallying scores and tattling on girls who show too much leg. It is about embracing a life of grace, his grace for you and me, overflowing to those around us. He calls us out of a life of hypocrisy, of saying all the right things and hiding our sins, and he says, "Do you want to keep pretending you are good? Or are you ready for me to live out my life through yours?"

The craziest thing is that when we own up to our rule loving, our pride, and our judging ways, we give Jesus a chance to change us, to begin his work of righteousness in our hearts and to fill us with mercy for those around us. He can free us from the bondage of rule following and set us on a path of loving him. He can give our blind eyes the vision to see him for who he is. Our Savior. This is our chance to break the rules in a good way. Let's not settle for Sunday school best or Pharisee-like piety—prettied up on the outside and dead on the inside. Let's follow Paul's lead and throw ourselves on the mercy of the One who loves us just as we are and let him do a work of grace within us. We will never regret it.

•

19

I Am a Wreck

When I was a kid, I remember my mom saying, "This house looks like the wreck of the *Hesperus*!" I had no idea what she meant. I just knew it wasn't good. A few years ago I found myself standing in the middle of my living room and declaring, "This house looks like the wreck of the *Hesperus*!" And I realized I still didn't know what it meant and I should look it up. So I did. Let's just say that Henry Wadsworth Longfellow was having a hard day when he wrote that poem. The "Wreck of the Hesperus" is about a sea captain who takes his daughter on a journey with him into a winter gale. The captain thinks he can weather any storm, but instead his frozen schooner, the *Hesperus*, splinters and shatters like glass on the reef of Norman's Woe. All are lost. It is a little depressing, to say the least, but it provides a vivid picture of my living room, metaphorically speaking. Socks in the middle of the floor. Crumbs in every corner. Surfaces littered with papers and toys. Complete chaos. Not a bad likening at all.

If I'm honest, it's not just my living room that looks like an encounter with the reef of Norman's Woe. There have been moments when my life has felt like the wreck of the *Hesperus*. Days when I didn't know up from down and my dreams were shattered. Moments when I couldn't possibly see how my life could ever be cohesive again. I've had times when I thought I would never see a day without tears. (Longfellow was not alone in his dark days, people. I've had quite a few of my own.)

I'll bet when Eve stepped foot out of the garden she felt her life was beyond salvage, hopeless and broken. I'm sure even Adam's reassurance couldn't calm her frayed nerves. I think she was probably scared out of her mind. It is in moments of complete brokenness that fear often takes flight in our souls. We become overwhelmed with anxiety and worry. Anxiety creeps in on soft feet and cripples us, filling our minds with doubt and what-ifs.

"Where is God?"

"Why am I hurting so much?"

"How can God love me when I am such a mess?"

"What if my life never gets better?"

"What if I get hurt like this again?"

"What if tomorrow is worse than today?"

You can easily see why we are wrecks when we think things like this. I hate the snake and his lies. He uses our hurts, missed opportunities, and life's tragedies to whip up fears, named and nameless, to get us to react. Many of us respond to life based on our fears. Just look at how many phobias there are in the dictionary. Hundreds upon hundreds. We are running scared. Even though many of us hide our fears really well under our filing systems and our peppy attitudes, underneath are wounded souls resembling the wreck of the *Hesperus*. Wind whipped and shattered.

Some of us try so hard to control our environment because something bad happened in our life and we never want to revisit that place again. We come up with ways to protect ourselves and do whatever we can to get away from that pain. Unfortunately, we get more freaked out when our coping mechanisms prove faulty, when the masks we wear and the power we try to wield over others and our circumstances don't work. Even more scary is the fear we have of God and how we think he will respond to our brokenness.

One deep fear keeps us far away from God: the ghastly and horrifying fear that God is done with us. We know he sees us for who we are. He knows how lousy we have been on more than one occasion. He knows we have tried everything in the book—from controlling to manipulating to regimenting our days in military fashion—to get the lives we think we need. He knows we are afraid he is through with us. We've had our shot and it's over. Just like Adam and Eve, we are about to get the boot. The snake preys on this fear. If he can keep us scared of the Creator, we will never learn of God's fantastic love for us.

Do you remember what God did when Adam and Eve left the garden? He told them that Eve was going to have pain in childbirth and that Adam would spend his days toiling in the fields. Then Genesis 3:21 says, "And the Lord God made clothing from animal skins for Adam and his wife." He made them clothes. He covered their shame and their nakedness. They had done the very thing he had asked them not to do, and God showed them mercy and love. They had wrought ruination on his immaculate world, and God was thinking about their well-being. Why would he do this? Why didn't he just smack them upside the head? Because he loved them in spite of themselves. He made them. He created them in his image. He cannot stop being who he is: a God of love.

Do you know that he has not changed? Since the time of Eden, his nature has not changed one whit. He pours out his love on us every day whether we accept it or not. He offered up his own Son to die in our place, so we could have a chance at a new life. What more does he have to do to show us he loves us? His love has nothing to do with whether or not we have messed up in the last twenty-four hours. It does not hinge on whether we have read the Bible in its entirety or ever lied to our mother. It does not even matter if our life is a shambles right at this moment. It has everything to do with his nature and his love for his children. While our minds cannot grasp this, it is the truth our hope rests on.

John, the disciple Jesus loved, says it best in 1 John 4:9–10: "God showed how much he loved us by sending his only Son into the world so that we might have eternal life through him. This is real love. It is not that we loved God, but that he loved us and sent his Son as a sacrifice to take away our sins."

He loves us. Really loves us. In the way a dad loves his kids. Naughty or good. Right or wrong. Happy or hurting. He loves all his kids, and he cannot stand to be separated from us. Arms flung open, he is calling out to us. "Kids! Get over here! I love you!"

As for earning his approval with our shipshape lives, he knows every one of us is a wreck. He is God, after all. If you are still wrestling with the fact that you can't get it all together, he has something to say about that too. You never will. Stop looking to yourself for your salvation. It's not going to happen. There is no new method that can put you back together again. You have to trust him to do that for you. And you can because he loves you so much. John continues on in verses 16–18:

> We know how much God loves us, and we have put our trust in him. God is love, and all who live in love live in God, and God lives in them. And as we live in God, our love grows more perfect. So we will not be afraid on the day of judgment, but we can face him with confidence because we are like Christ here in this world. Such love has no fear because perfect love expels all fear. If we are afraid, it is for fear of judgment, and this shows that his love has not been perfected in us.

On that day when we stand before God, souls bared, wrecked and all, we don't have to be afraid. Our confidence comes not from the fact that we are good or our lives were unblemished. It comes from the fact that we are God's children. John says that if we are running scared from God, it's because we don't know how much he loves us. We can stand steady in his love, and our fear can take a hike. Throughout Scripture, God tells his people over and over again, "Don't be afraid." He is not a fan of the fear that has ruled us and woven itself into the fabric of our beings, the fear that has riddled our thoughts and weighed on our hearts. That comes from the snake. And as we know, the snake has been defeated. (Good riddance!)

God would have us know his love, the kind of love that hides a sinner's shame and sets a plan of redemption in place. As we submit our lives to God's love, to his care, he will change us. He will salvage what we never thought could be salvaged. There is not a wreck that is worthless to him. He is not a duct-tape kind of God, piecing our lives together in a mishmash sort of way. No, he has always been in the healing business. He will breathe new life into our souls with the power of his Holy Spirit. He will reshape our lives with his capable hands, binding up broken hearts, casting out fear, extending new mercies every morning. I don't know about you, but I'm in, wreck of the *Hesperus* and all.

20

I Am in Denial

I am in denial about a lot of things, the least of which is that my neck skin is starting to look weird. I'm praying it is the lighting in my bathroom. I'm in denial that my memory is shot, even though I often can't remember people's names. I'm in denial about the fact that I live along the San Andreas Fault and that at any time we could experience the "big one." That would be the earthquake that dumps California into the Pacific and leaves Nevada with a lovely coastline. But mostly I'm in denial about the amount of control I have in my life. I like to think I can run my life like a well-oiled machine. I like to think I can do so without help. In reality, things are pretty much a gong show around here. And I would be lying if I said I don't need divine intervention on a daily basis.

In the last two months, there have been household disasters, moth infestations, writer's block, and anger. (That would be anger on my part.) There have been a back injury, copious drugs for the back injury, work issues, and church dilemmas. There have been an angry uprising by the five-year-old (he thinks he owns the world), an ignoring of all rules by the eight-year-old (he thinks the world revolves around him), and some preteen angst from the ten-year-old (he thinks the world is against him.) On all fronts, it seems I am not in any way, shape, or form in control of my life. And the craziest part? That is the truth of it. I am not in control of my life. This becomes clear to me when I have to do a deep-knee squat to unload the dishwasher, holding my back in an upright position. I can't handle my own vertebrae, let alone my life. On the bright side, my thighs are growing stronger by the day, an unexpected bonus in my wacky, out-of-control world.

Sometimes God chooses to pry our manipulative fingers off the so-called steering wheel of life by using the school of hard knocks. Not that he visits tragedy upon us. Rather, he chooses to use every wild situation or simple annoyance that makes up our lives to remind us who is in control. It doesn't take much heartache (or back pain, for that matter) to remind us that we don't get to dictate what our lives are like. Sometimes life flips us head over heels, and we are caught off guard, looking for a soft place to land. That soft place is the palm of God's hand. He will hold us close and wipe our tears if we will let him. He will light a path for us and bring us home if we ask him to. He will show up and shatter our expectations if we will let go of our preconceived ideas and throw a desperate prayer up to the heavens. "God, I need you!" Or, "I want to believe in you! Help me!" It is when we begin to admit our great need for him that he is most able to work in us. To fortify us with his love. To calm our ambitions with his peace. To weave a bit of joy and hope into our souls.

In James 4:7–10, James has a firm word for the Jewish Christians. He is not pulling any punches with this portion of his letter.

> So humble yourselves before God. Resist the Devil, and he will flee from you. Draw close to God, and God will draw close to you. Wash your hands, you sinners; purify your hearts, you hypocrites. Let there be tears for the wrong things you have done. Let there be sorrow and deep grief. Let there be sadness instead of laughter, and gloom instead of joy. When you bow down before the Lord and admit your dependence on him, he will lift you up and give you honor.

I am a person who likes uplifting verses. Healing words and gentle encouragement go a long way with me. Most of my devotional reading leans toward the psalms and the teachings of Jesus. You won't find me spending a whole lot of time in Leviticus or Haggai. So I tend to shrink back when James starts calling out the hypocrites and sinners, telling them to cast off their joy, weep for the wrongs they have done, and get their acts together. It offends me a bit. But I think James is telling it like it is. When we are caught up in life, ignoring God or pretending we don't need God, we are saying, "In my own strength, wisdom, forbearance, etc., I know all I need to know to get on with this life, and I don't need you." We may not think this is what we are saying, but our actions speak far louder than our words. If we are pursuing perfectionism or trying to control the outcome of our lives, we are not pursuing our Creator or letting him work out what he desires in us.

James is giving the Jewish Christians a wake-up call here. He's trying to get their attention so they will reevaluate how they are living before it all goes woefully wrong for them.

He is trying to shake them out of their denial. In essence, James is saying (my paraphrase here), "Get over yourself. He is God. You aren't. Don't mess around with the snake. If you get close to God, he will get close to you. If you're messing around, knock it off! If you are saying one thing and doing another, cut it out! If you've blown it, own it and confess. Quit joking around and get serious about it. Stop pretending you don't need the God of the universe to restore your life. When you tell him how much you depend on him, he will hold you high and honor you!"

James knows his readers are offtrack, and he loves them too much to let them lose out on the life God has for them. Sometimes I get offtrack and I need someone to set me straight. God put Scott in my life for that very reason. He calls me out regularly, not because he is petty or takes pleasure in making me feel small but because he loves me. He loves me a lot. He wants me to be more than I am at present. He wants me to be the woman God designed me to be. I do the same for him. God often allows people in our lives, circumstances that shake us, and his sovereign Word to get our attention. When we get to a place in our lives where we think that we have attained an Eden of our making or that we can control the outcome of our days, we are mistaken. When we are in denial about needing God's daily grace and intervention in our lives, we are walking away from God. He's not about to let this happen. He loves us too much. We are his children, after all. So he shouts out across the fields of stars he formed: "I am the One who loves you. You need me. Don't forget that! Let me take you in my arms and hold you high! I want to wash over you with my grace and show you off."

I love the word picture of God lifting us up. It reminds me of something my dad used to do with Will when he was a baby. My dad would take Will by the shins and lift him up in the air above his head. Will, by some innate baby knowledge, would lock his legs, straighten his body, and grin his drooly baby grin as Dad walked him around the room. He had complete confidence in my dad. Will knew there was no way in the world Grandpa was going to drop him. He could get higher and see more when he was in my dad's capable hands, and he loved it. (Never mind the fact that I used to call out, "Dad, put him down! You are making me nervous!")

When we are in God's hands, we get to see more and get higher than we ever thought possible. We can have complete confidence in him. When we get close to God, our entire perspective changes. We can own up to who we are (sinners miraculously saved by grace) and let him do the deep work that needs to be done in our lives. Hands free. Held up by the boundless grace of our Creator. Basking in his presence. Even when we don't understand the whys and how-comes of our lives.

So take James's words to heart. Not in a you're-no-good-and-you-messed-up kind of way but in a get-as-close-as-you-can-to-God-and-let-him-do-the-heavy-lifting kind of way. He is the proud papa wanting to show off the beauty of his children. That would be your beauty and mine. He wants the world to see the beauty of his grace flowing through our lives as we begin to trust the One who made us. The loveliness of a burgeoning hope that is welling up within us and overtaking our fears and anxieties. The wonder of mercy after mercy anchoring us in the belief that he loves us like crazy, mess and all. And the enormity of his love filling our souls, pervading the dailiness of our lives, the craziness of our circumstances, and the depth of our dreams. All because we have found our way back to a life soaked in his presence. It's never too late to run to him, arms flung high, and admit we need him now more than ever. Without him, there is not much to see in life. He can't wait to lift us up in his everlasting arms and squeeze us close. That is what dads do best. Especially heavenly ones.

21

I Need a New Idea of What Perfect Looks Like

I was five years old when I got my first pair of glasses. I failed an eye test at school, and the next thing I knew I was picking out rainbow-colored frames at the local eye doctor's office. I am extremely nearsighted. Anytime anyone who knows anything about eyes sees my prescription, they say things like, "Sweet mercy!" or "Bless your heart!" That is never encouraging. Once I was wearing my glasses and a friend told me, "You might want to get some new glasses. They have special lenses now so that your eyeglasses don't look so thick." I gave her a withering look and said, "These *are* those special lenses." She's hasn't mentioned my coke-bottle glasses since.

Usually, I wear contacts because I have much better peripheral vision with them . . . and because no one screams, "My word, you have thick glasses!" when I'm wearing them. I've always gotten my contacts from my mom's cousin Gary, who is an optometrist. A few years back I asked him, "Tell me the truth. How bad are my eyes?"

He said, "You're blind."

I knew it before he said it. The only time I am without contacts or glasses is when I am sleeping. My children often wake me with the words, "Mom, can you see me?" They know that unless our noses are touching they are faceless blobs to me. Faceless blobs that I love, of course. Being extremely nearsighted causes you to realize three things: (1) your ability to judge things is impaired (is that a building or a truck?), (2) your view of reality is distorted (everything is blurry), and (3) you need help to manage your world (Lasik surgery, glasses, contacts, or small children who are willing to fetch and carry can do the trick).

I have recently begun to suspect that I am equally myopic when it comes to my spiritual vision. Despite my best efforts, it can be difficult to decipher the path God has laid out before me. Just like Adam and Eve after they ate the fruit, my eyes have been opened. And not in a good way. My idea of perfect and right and good is not naturally the same idea God has of perfect and right and good. It's as if the Eden gene has skewed the way I see life, how I view God, and how I interpret who he intended me to be. My friend Marty says we were born with the taste of the fruit in our mouths. We're so Eve-ish in how we see life and all it offers us that we don't see eye to eye with God on how our lives should play out. We survey everything through a self-centered lens. Even when we try to get it right, we mess up. Our perception of a good life is not necessarily God's perception of a good life.

How can we possibly see straight? Are there some holy contact lenses out there that can clarify life for us? Or a stylish pair of biblical goggles that can change our worldview? I'm sorry to say the answer is no on both accounts. Nor is there a trained canine that can help us find God's way for us. The only thing that makes a difference in how we view life is an encounter with the One who heals the blind. Everything hinges on Jesus. Everything. Without him we are in the dark, wandering hopelessly, looking for something to shed light on our paths in this world.

Lucky for us, Jesus has a soft spot for blind people. He knows how devastating living in the dark is. For those alive in Jesus's day, blindness meant a limited and bleak existence. Jesus went out of his way to heal the blind. In John 9, Jesus healed a blind man. He made some mud using his spit and dirt and put it on the man's eyes. Jesus sent him to the pool of Siloam to wash, and the man came back with perfect vision. This ticked off the religious community because Jesus healed him on the Sabbath, showing a complete disregard for the proper etiquette of the Lord's Day. The Pharisees were so whipped up that they called the formerly blind man and his parents in for questioning. They wanted to convince themselves that Jesus was demon possessed or at least a sinner and could not possibly be from God. When questioned, the man said, "Never since the world began has anyone been able to open the eyes of someone born blind. If this man were not from God, he couldn't do it" (John 9:32–33). This really irritated the Pharisees, and they threw him out of the temple. Then things started to get exciting. The Bible says:

> When Jesus heard what had happened, he found the man and said, "Do you believe in the Son of Man?"
>
> The man answered, "Who is he, sir, because I would like to."

> "You have seen him," Jesus said, "and he is speaking to you!"
>
> "Yes, Lord," the man said, "I believe!" And he worshiped Jesus.
>
> Then Jesus told him, "I have come to judge the world. I have come to give sight to the blind and to show those who think they see that they are blind."
>
> The Pharisees who were standing there heard him and asked, "Are you saying we are blind?"
>
> "If you were blind, you wouldn't be guilty," Jesus replied. "But you remain guilty because you claim you can see." (John 9:35–41)

The blind man knew he was blind. No doubt about it. His entire life he had stumbled around in the dark, seeking a hand to guide him or a person to save him. Jesus did that for him in a moment. With a fist full of mud, he revolutionized this man's world. But he didn't stop there. Jesus was concerned with more than the state of his retinas; he was also concerned about the state of his soul. Jesus asked him if he believed in the Son of Man. And when the man asked who he was, Jesus said, "It's me!" I wonder if the man lit up with joy at Jesus's words. He had heard his voice when Jesus had directed him to the pool. He had felt Jesus's fingers smooth mud over his eyes. But at this moment, he realized his healer stood before him, the only One who had ever offered him hope and a new life, the only One who had shut out the darkness and filled his eyes with light. If he wanted a Savior, there he was. And he wasn't going to miss his chance. He told Jesus, "Yes, Lord, I believe!" and worshiped him on the spot. He was in the presence of the One who was before time. He would never see things the same again with his eyes or his soul. They had both been touched by the God of the universe.

In the background of this scene are the Pharisees, who thought they had cornered the market on God and righteousness. They studied God their entire lives. They knew God. Or did they? The Pharisees were the perfectionists of their day. Their lives centered around holiness and rightness. They set about pleasing God by carefully grooming their lives and their holier-than-thou attitudes. And when Jesus showed up on their front porch, they were at a loss as to what to do with him. They would have liked to have kicked him into kingdom come. But instead, Jesus called them out, pointing out their inability to see him for who he was. Revealing their pride and their guilt. Accusing them of missing the point of who God is and how transformative his message is. They were spiritually blind, and they didn't get it. The Pharisees were clueless that they needed a healer as much as the blind man did.

It all comes down to this. Are you more like the blind man or the Pharisees? Are you ready for a new way of seeing things? Are you willing to put up with a little mud in your eye for a chance at the life you were designed for? Do you know who your Healer is? Do you recognize his voice? Have you felt his fingertips on the blind eyes of your soul? The healing, the revitalization of our spiritual eyes, can come only when we ask for it. The restoration in our vision can happen only when we recognize Jesus for who he is. Son of God. Messiah. Healer. Bearer of Light.

All along we may have said, "I want to know God. I want to follow his ways." And that is good. But the Pharisees did that, and their actions, their self-righteousness, and their love of sticking to their rules led to Christ's crucifixion. But the blind man, humble, owning his stuff, throwing himself on the mercy of the Christ and his healing power, believed and was set free. New eyes. New life. New way of living.

Jesus can do the same for us. When we turn our back on our inner Pharisee and own up to our blindness and our inability to navigate this journey of life without him, Jesus doesn't hold back. When we ask for a new way of looking at life, he is more than happy to oblige. He will turn our world upside down and inside out with his light and love and will set us on a path of hope and freedom. A path that is found only when we keep our eyes fixed on him. A path of believing, worshiping, and following the only One who can give sight to the blind. I think it's time for some new eyes. Are you with me?

22

I Am Not in Control

When I published my first book, I thought the heavens had opened up. I was living out the dream I had dreamt as a little girl. An actual book had my name on the cover. Unbelievable. I was ready for it all—the book signings, the blog tours, the book launch party. I couldn't wait. But something else happened when I got published that I wasn't ready for. Something that plucked at a deep-rooted fear within me. A fear that made my mouth go dry and my mind go blank. People thought that because I had written a book I could speak. Publicly. Now, I am positively brilliant at speaking at home. I can hand down dictates to my children like nobody's business. But to get up in front of people I don't know and declare the Word of the Lord? Not on your life.

I have always wanted to be fearless. Like Amelia Earhart. Winging into the unknown, breathless with anticipation for what tomorrow holds. But in reality, I am much more like Emily Dickinson, willing to let my words speak for me as I stick close to my comfort zone. Public speaking is not my comfort zone. It is my un-comfort zone. It is also my let's-see-how-quickly-I-can-sweat-through-my-clothes zone. When our good friend Mark Batterson, from National Community Church in Washington, DC, emailed me about speaking on Mother's Day weekend in 2009, I immediately began sweating. Mind you, I was just sitting at the computer by myself and my palms got slick. The plan was that NCC would fly the entire family out, and I would speak three times in three locations. As I finished reading the email, I began to feel light-headed and thought that maybe the Lord was calling me home right then and there.

I talked to Scott, and he was excited. He said of course he knew I could do it. He told me I wasn't just a writer, I was a communicator. (Clearly, he sees things for what they are not yet.) Then I called my brother-in-law Van for advice. Van had asked me to speak earlier that year at his church, Willamette Christian Center, and I had been noncommittal. My question to him had been, "Do you mean in big church?" (You can see that my fear had claimed me, since I reverted to child-speak while talking to Van.) Van had said, "Yes. In big church." Then he had laughed at me. I told Van I didn't know what to do, and he said, "Sue, I think God has some things he would like to say through you."

That broke me down because I thought God did have some things to say through me. But that was why I had written a book. There are no rewrites or edits in public speaking, people. So I prayed. That is always a good thing to do when you are sweaty and wracked with fear. As I prayed, I got the distinct sense that God was opening a door that he wanted me to walk through. I looked at the pros and cons. The pros: if I went, I would be saying no to my fear and yes to God.

I would be letting go of my control issues and letting God work through me. And we would get to spend some quality time with people we really love. The cons: there might not be enough deodorant in the tristate area to deal with the amount of sweat I would produce. And then there was the chance I would fail miserably and humiliate myself, my family, and Mark all in one fell swoop. Yep, there was that.

I knew I could say no but that I would miss out on something God had for me. So I emailed Mark and said, "Yes." And then he emailed me back and said, "Great!" and, "Would you be willing to speak at a women's night as well?" I emailed back, "Yes." Then I promptly put my head down on my kitchen table and bawled. Like a baby. Because how in the world could I do it? How could I stand in front of hundreds of people and talk? Four times in one weekend, no less. How could it be done? It felt completely out of my control. And it was.

When Jesus died on the cross, he gave us access to a relationship with God the Creator and a chance at a new way of living, a way of living in which we realign ourselves with God and let him be the one in control of our lives. Some of us assume that this yielding of control happens automatically upon recitation of the sinner's prayer. We thought we would say, "I believe that Jesus is the Son of God and died on the cross for my sins," and then presto, we would be completely changed and would never struggle again with fear or doubt or over-perspiring. You would think. But just like Eve had a choice (to bite or not to bite) in the garden, we have a choice every day in every situation that comes our way. Do we choose to play it safe, or do we hand over our lives to the living God? Are we going to yield control of our lives to the Creator, or are we going to stick to the old well-worn path of control issues and perfectionism? The apostle Paul puts it this way in Romans 6:12–14:

> Do not let sin control the way you live; do not give in to its lustful desires. Do not let any part of your body become a tool of wickedness, to be used for sinning. Instead, give yourselves completely to God since you have been given new life. And use your whole body as a tool to do what is right for the glory of God. Sin is no longer your master, for you are no longer subject to the law, which enslaves you to sin. Instead, you are free by God's grace.

This is the choice. We can say, "Thank you for the saving and all, but I still want to run my own life, even though it is pathetic and I don't have a whole lot of power at my fingertips. I am used to calling the shots." Or we can say to God, "I want you to be in control of my life. Period. All those weaknesses that hound me, all those worries and selfish motives, I'm giving them to you. Whatever shots you want to call, those are the ones I am going with." The only way to gain the new life of freedom we so desperately long for is by giving ourselves completely to God.

It is a lot to take in for one who likes to control things. Yielding our lives also goes against the grain of the perfectionist, the manipulator, and the sneak in us. It is a deliberate giving up of old ways. But there is no way around it. There is no straddling fences here. Do you or do you not want to be free from your old patterns, your control issues, and your manhandling ways? Okay, then. Take a deep breath with me and say it: I am not in control. I don't want to be in control. God, I give myself to you completely.

Now breathe again. How do you feel? Unmoored? Weird? Adrift? Untethered?

I'm thinking that what you are experiencing, what has left you feeling a little at odds with your normal self, is called freedom. Yep, that would be freedom.

You have effectively relinquished control. And while it may seem unfamiliar and uncomfortable, you are in a good place. This place may make you feel like you want to bawl. You know, lay your head down and weep for the unknown that lies before you. You may be thinking, "I lied. I want to be in control again." I know this feeling of desperation from experience, but I assure you that you are exactly where you need to be. You have just spoken the truth for the first time in a long time. You admitted out loud that you aren't in control. It's a shock to the system, isn't it? Despite what you may think, you have never had the ability to order your own steps. You do not have the ability to move mountains or to determine what will happen an hour from now. You cannot be sinless or perfect or unblemished on your own. You do not have the ability to see through time to the future or to redeem the past. I'm sorry to burst your bubble. But the beauty of this moment is that you recognize something in yourself. You see that you have a chance at a new way of living, and you are going to take it. You have chosen to let the One who has all the control do something with your life.

Paul goes on to say in Romans 7:4–6:

> So this is the point: The law no longer holds you in its power, because you died to its power when you died with Christ on the cross. And now you are united with the one who was raised from the dead. As a result, you can produce good fruit, that is, good deeds for God. When we were controlled

> by our old nature, sinful desires were at work within us, and the law aroused these evil desires that produced sinful deeds, resulting in death. But now we have been released from the law, for we died with Christ, and we are no longer captive to its power. Now we can really serve God, not in the old way by obeying the letter of the law, but in the new way, by the Spirit.

When we decide to turn our back on the lure of the Eden gene and the whispers of the snake, when we decide to submit every part of our lives to God, something shifts. That would be the seat of power. We recognize that only God has the power to change us. When we relinquish control to him, we begin living in a new way, by the Spirit. I know you are thinking, "Yes! That is fantastic!" But you may also be thinking, "What in the world does that mean?"

It means you will be living the life you were designed for, a life in which the Creator has free rein to eradicate your fears and forgive your sins and birth new hopes and dreams in your soul. It means you will begin to recognize the voice of the One who loves you most. It means that each day as the battle between the old nature (controlling, conniving, selfish) and the new nature (loving, forgiving, selfless) wages within, God is on your side, rooting you on, making his will known through his Holy Spirit, and giving you the ability to choose rightly. It means that the old you will begin to give way to the new you, the person you long to be, one moment, one choice, one prayer at a time. It does not mean you will be perfect. It does not mean you will not have moments of panic. But it does mean that the God of the universe has stepped in and taken over the work of molding and shaping you, the work of moving within you and making your paths straight. (Helpful hint: be aware that straight paths can make you sweaty. I'm just being honest.)

For the record, Mother's Day weekend at National Community Church went off without a hitch. Other than a case of hair gone wild due to intense humidity, a bout of allergies that fogged my contacts, and a battle with an errant microphone that didn't want to stay on my head, I would call it a high victory—a moment when God met me amid my fear and weakness and became my help and my strong tower. Speaking four times in one weekend was a baptism by fire. And I am not the same person I was because of it. Because now I know the truth: when we place our lives in the hands of the Creator, we become more than we could ever dream to be on our own. In a time and place when I could not do something myself, God came through. And, my friends, it absolutely does not get any better than that.

23

I Need a Paradigm Shift

On Valentine's Day this year, our family went around the dinner table and told each person one thing we liked about him or her. This can be difficult for boys. They like to give rude examples, like how loud someone can burp. But we gave firm instructions that only serious answers were allowed. I told Jack I liked the way he is compassionate toward people. Addie told me that he liked that I snuggle with him. When we got to Will, he looked expectantly at Scott. Scott told him, "Will, I like the way you draw." Will is talented with colored pencils. Will smiled and then got up and moved around the table and whispered in Scott's ear, "Dad, I thought you were going to say that you liked me because I am Scott Jr.!"

Will resembles his dad in a variety of ways. His curly blond hair. The shape of his hands and his forearms. His wiry frame. His love of music. His obsession with drawing cartoons. The way his teeth are spaced in the front. The blue of his eyes. These things all mirror Scott. One of Scott's prouder parental moments was when Will dropped down and did the centipede dance move across the living room floor, just like his dad. Scott shed a tear of joy. Whenever Will does something that is reminiscent of Scott, he announces with pride, "I'm Scott Jr." Will loves being like his dad because as far as he is concerned, his dad is the best. Which is why he wanted to remind his dad on Valentine's Day that he is just a smaller version of the man he loves most in the world.

There is something pretty unique about the father-son relationship. The kinship. The foundational sense of knowing where you came from and who loves you best. Fathers and sons long to be proud of each other. I think Jesus feels no different about God the Father. Everything that is important to the Father is important to Jesus. All the characteristics found in God are found in Jesus. Jesus represents his Father completely. All that power and holiness, all that grace and mercy wrapped up in human form mirror the heavenly Father. Jesus and his Father are one and the same.

Jesus told his disciples in John 14:7, "If you had known who I am, then you would have known who my Father is. From now on you know him and have seen him!" This must have been completely mind-blowing to the disciples. They saw the face of God when they looked into Jesus's eyes. The One so pure, so all-powerful, whom no one had ever laid eyes on, stood before them. Like Father like Son. It rocked their world. They caught a firsthand glimpse of the God who had created them.

Sometimes when we read about Jesus's relationship with the Father, how he knows beyond a shadow of a doubt that he is doing his Father's bidding, we can get a little jealous. We wish we could be that sure of our relationship with God. We wish we knew God as well as Jesus does. But do you know what is crazy? We're not the only ones wishing that. The Creator God is so keen on that happening that he made a way for it to be possible. We just can't wrap our minds around it.

Paul tells the Romans that Christ has done an amazing thing. When we are made right with God through Jesus, the same Spirit that raised Christ from the dead lives in us, and just as God's Spirit raised Christ from the dead, he will give life to our mortal bodies. We are no longer slaves to our sin nature. In fact, not only are we not slaves to sin but we are also God's children. God wants us to have a father-child relationship. Romans 8:14–16 says, "For all who are led by the Spirit of God are children of God. So you should not be like cowering, fearful slaves. You should behave instead like God's very own children, adopted into his family—calling him 'Father, dear Father.' For his Holy Spirit speaks to us deep in our hearts and tells us that we are God's children."

In our Eve-ishness, sometimes it is hard to believe we are God's children. His sons and daughters. We can't imagine approaching him that way. You know, the way kids run up to their dad, throw their arms around his neck, feel completely at ease hanging out with him. We can't reconcile our control issues, our perfectionism, or our sins with the truth. We think we have to ingratiate ourselves to God, that we have to punish ourselves or beat our sinful nature into submission before he will accept us. In actuality, that has already been done. It happened on the cross. When we invite Jesus into our lives, we no longer follow in Adam and Eve's footsteps, hiding behind bushes and blaming each other. The paradigm shift comes when we realize we are following in Jesus's footsteps and he leads us into a new relationship with our heavenly Father.

When Jesus decided to give his life for our sins and bridge the gap between us and the Father, he didn't just right the wrong that happened in the garden. He didn't just undo what happened with Adam and Eve. He invited us to be a part of his family. By adoption, we get to take on the family name. We get to know the Father in a way that only a kid can know his dad. You are probably thinking, "That's crazy! God doesn't really love me as much as he loves Jesus!" But he does. Just as Adam and Eve were created in God's image, Jesus makes a way for us to be made in our Creator's image again. From the inside out. As God's Spirit moves in us, a funny thing happens. We start to look like him. We speak like him and act like him. We laugh about the things that tickle him and weep over the things that break his heart. Not because of anything we have done but because God's Spirit is in us.

Because of our Eden gene and our desire to do things our own way, we keep trying to get on God's good side. In reality, we are already on his good side. He considers us his children. I'm his kid. You're his kid. He's our dad. We have already read Romans 8:28, which says, "And we know that God causes everything to work together for the good of those who love God and are called according to his purpose for them." But look how the apostle Paul continues on:

> For God knew his people in advance, and he chose them to become like his Son, so that his Son would be the firstborn, with many brothers and sisters. And having chosen them, he called them to come to him. And he gave them right standing with himself, and he promised them his glory. What can we say about such wonderful things as these? If God is for us, who can ever be against us? Since God did not spare even his

> own Son but gave him up for us all, won't God, who gave us Christ, also give us everything else? (Rom. 8:29–32)

It's true. All the good, the bad, and the ugly of your life can be used for God's glory when you are in his family. He chose you. He called you. He knows you. Every nuance of your personality, every thought in your mind, every desire in your heart are known to him. He's given you a place in his family. He is making a junior out of you. If he loves you enough to give up his own Son on your behalf, how much more does he have in store for you? The possibilities are endless. You don't have to win him over. Even now his Holy Spirit is working in you, making you over in his image, shaping your soul with his goodness and grace. He is on your side. He's rooting for you. There is only one thing left for you to do.

Believe it.

24

I Am Ready for a New Out-of-Control Me

This year for my birthday Scott got me a bike. And it's not just any bike. It's a beach-cruiser bike with fat wheels and a sweet basket hanging from the handlebars and . . . wait for it . . . a cup holder. (The fact that the beverage in the cup holder spritzes your upper thigh with each bump in the road is neither here nor there. It has a cup holder, people.) That bike calls out to everything girlish in me. I feel about six years old when I am riding it down the street. When the breeze whips across my face and the whir of the wheels zipping on the asphalt fills my ears, I can't help but laugh. If you see a woman careening wildly down the streets of Redwood City giggling like a kindergartner while sipping on a beverage, that would be me.

But when I remember what it was like learning how to ride a bike, two images come to mind: wobbly wheels and scraped knees. Climbing onto a two-wheeler for the first time often leaves one gripped with fear. I remember hoping that when my dad let go I would, by some miracle of momentum and balance, be able to keep myself upright, lest I pitch into the juniper bushes in front of our house. I hate juniper bushes. They are so poky. (I think they are a result of the fall for sure.) And wouldn't you know it, when my dad let go, I fell . . . more than once. I scraped all the skin off my palms. I left my bike's imprint on a juniper bush or three. I cried. But I didn't let those wobbles and crashes stop me. The hope of riding free on a big-girl bike far outweighed the fear of the falls.

Unbridled hope has to squelch the fear of the unknown to motivate us to action before we can ever be more than we are. The lure of riding free on two wheels has to outweigh the fear of the dreaded junipers . . . and scratched palms . . . and scabbed-over knees. And the lure of living free, with God's Spirit given free rein in our hearts and minds, has to outweigh the fears of giving over control and of centering ourselves around his will instead of our own. We fool ourselves into thinking it is scarier to put our lives in God's hands when really it is far scarier to take our lives into our own hands. (Note to self: remember Eve.) We were made for a life of relying on him. We were made to live free. Because of Jesus we can. All we have to do is give ourselves over to God. Now, mind you, you will probably have to do this several times a day . . . or twice an hour . . . depending on how much of a control freak or perfectionist you are. But don't be discouraged. The more you do it, the more you will see him begin to work on your behalf.

Imagine yourself turning your back on your sin nature, your Eve-ishness, that thing in you that craves control and perfection and, palms up, turning over your life to the Creator God, asking that his Holy Spirit begin to change you, to lead you, to guide you. Paul put it to the Romans like this:

> And so, dear Christian friends, I plead with you to give your bodies to God. Let them be a living and holy sacrifice—the kind he will accept. When you think of what he has done for you, is this too much to ask? Don't copy the behavior and customs of this world, but let God transform you into a new person by changing the way you think. Then you will know what God wants you to do, and you will know how good and pleasing and perfect his will really is. (Rom. 12:1–2)

Now, you may feel your perfectionist self get agitated over the "living and holy sacrifice" part of that passage, thinking that somehow you have to make yourself alive and holy. And that may segue into thinking, "Oh, dear Lord! I completely forgot my morning devotions for the last three days," and then you decide to give up all together. But did you perchance notice that the only perfect thing mentioned in this verse is God's will? There was no mention of you as far as I can see. So take a deep breath. Remember that the holy and living part of yourself is the power of the cross working itself out in you and not something that you conjure up. (That takes a load off, doesn't it?) The Creator God wants to transform you, starting with your mind. In the past, you may have thought, "I will never be perfect." Now God will bring to mind the thought, "While I was yet a sinner Christ died for me." In the past, you may have struggled with working your way into God's good graces. Now he will remind you that his grace is sufficient for you and his power is made perfect in your weakness. And when you yield control to him and then take it back and then re-yield it, feeling like a failure all the while, he will remind you that he will be faithful to carry out the work he began in you. Because he can.

Some people (me, in particular) forget that this journey of following Jesus is also a fight. Not a fight to get free from all our issues on our own but a daily fight to choose God instead of ourselves so that God can move in our lives. A fight to say no to our sin nature and yes to God's Spirit within us so that he can do the things that only he can do. It is a fight to turn toward the Father and then let him do the rest. We're throwing everything down—our problems, our issues, our hopes, our capabilities—and it is up to him to make something of them. Once we let go of everything, it's all on him. Isn't that refreshing? It is our job to choose him. It is his job to free us from ourselves and form us and breathe new life into us.

Only when we offer ourselves up can God begin to transform us. When that begins to happen, "then you will know what God wants you to do, and you will know how good and pleasing and perfect his will really is" (Rom. 12:2). Knowing can come only after letting go. That seems counterintuitive, doesn't it? Think of it as the anti-Eden gene. Anti-Eve-ishness. Anti-snake. Letting go may not come intuitively, but as you practice putting yourself, your day, your will into God's hands, it will begin to feel right.

My friend Marty knows all about letting go and putting her life in God's hands. We are alike in a lot of ways. She's a pastor's wife, a mom of three, and a marriage and family counselor. I am a pastor's wife, a mom of three, and I need a marriage and family counselor. We both like to decorate our houses, read good books, and eat dark chocolate. And we may have struggled a time or twelve with perfectionism and control issues in our lives. To me she is Beautiful Marty, since that is what her husband, Shane, called her even before they started dating. A few years ago Marty found out she had a brain tumor, and everything in her world tilted. Even though it was benign, its removal caused her to lose her hearing in one ear and affected the nerves on one side of her face, which affected her eye, her smile, and her balance.

I asked Marty the other day about her surgery, and she told me that she found healing in her hardship. All those things she struggled with—the perfectionism, the control issues, how she felt about herself—shifted after the surgery. It was as if when the tumor came out, so did her malignant thinking. Her need for perfection and control. Her need to have her life look a certain way. She said God literally had to do brain surgery to change her thinking. We laughed at that. And then she said she hopes God doesn't heal her face all the way if doing so would make her forget all she has learned in this process. That made me cry. Because I want to be like Marty when I grow up. To let God work in me even when it hurts. To know his strength in my weak places. To get free of old thinking and let God transform my mind. It's funny, but Marty's healing seems to spread to those she talks to, changing hearts and transforming minds. She is passing the freedom along.

There is freedom when we let go of ourselves and hold fast to the Father. Jesus did this moment by moment while on this earth. Each breath was a perpetual reminder that he was on earth to do the Father's will. Even when it felt so wrong, when he was tormented in the Garden of Gethsemane, praying about the torture of the cross that lay before him, he told the Father, "Not my will but yours."

He did not utter those words so that in turn we could fritter away our lives, running willy-nilly through life, controlling others, setting impossible standards for ourselves, or making lame, half-brained decisions. He uttered those words so we could be free. He uttered those words so that the power of the Holy Spirit could take hold of our hearts and reside in our souls. So that his life and breath could dwell in us. All we have to do is call out to him, saying something like, "My life is yours in its entirety. I'm not keeping it to myself for another minute." And as Paul says so eloquently, "When you think of what he has done for you, is this too much to ask?"

Nope, it isn't. He offered his perfect life up for our salvation, and we in return give him our broken lives. Our issues and our sins. Our harbored hatreds and our prized possessions. Our neatly organized schedules and our carefully charted running logs. Our spreadsheets and our game plans. Our pains and our secret fears. Our childhood passions and our greatest hopes. And in return he sets us free—to do and be and become all that he designed us to be. Jesus said it himself: "The thief's [i.e., the snake's] purpose is to steal and kill and destroy. My purpose is to give life in all its fullness" (John 10:10). Really, what we crave more than anything is a full, rich life of knowing and loving Jesus and having him know and love us.

So the decision lies with us. As it did with Eve. And Adam. And Sarah. And Rebekah. And Naomi. And every other human being shaped in the image of God who has walked this good earth. Are you ready to make the choice? Are you ready to live in expectancy of what he has for you and offer your everything up to him? Are you ready to brave your fears of letting go to see what magnificence may lie in the future when God takes control of your life? Or will you turn back? Keep to the safety of the known? Believe snaky lies and make the same Eve-ish choices you have always made, limiting what

God can do in your life by your own capabilities and your lack of foresight? Will you do what comes naturally, giving in to the Eden gene? Or will you embrace the new life that the power of the cross has wrought within you and yield to the One who can give you wings?

Just in case you are not sure, wavering a bit, wondering if he might not know how to navigate your path or care for you in the manner to which you are accustomed, Isaiah, a man who gave his life to being a mouthpiece for the Most High, has a word for you:

> He will feed his flock like a shepherd. He will carry the lambs in his arms, holding them close to his heart. He will gently lead the mother sheep with their young.
>
> Who else has held the oceans in his hand? Who has measured off the heavens with his fingers? Who else knows the weight of the earth or has weighed out the mountains and the hills? Who is able to advise the Spirit of the LORD? Who knows enough to be his teacher or counselor? (Isa. 40:11–13)

Making a conscious decision to place your life in the hands of the One who measured off the heavens with his fingers is never a bad call.

He is I am that I am.
The Alpha and the Omega.
The Beginning and the End.
The Provider.
The Deliverer.
The Way.
The Truth.

The Life.
The Bright and Morning Star.
The Path Straightener.
The Grace Giver.
The Mind Renewer.
The Heart Strengthener.

And the list of his awesomeness goes on and on and on.

Let an unshakable faith in the Creator God surge up within you and set you free. Fling fear to the wind and let the hope of all that you can be in him propel you into a new, unleashed life as the power of God's Holy Spirit begins a new work within you. A training-wheels-off, hair-whipping-in-the-wind, exhilarating kind of work. A work of shaping you into the image of the One you were meant to resemble in the first place. He is waiting even now to take all that you are offering him. To grab you up in his arms, calm your fears, and give you wings to soar. So what are you waiting for?

Conclusion

The New Perfect

The very fact that you have finished reading this book speaks to your persevering nature. (Give yourself an air high five! Good job!) And that very nature is going to stand you in good stead as you embark on your new adventure of freedom and following Jesus, because, more likely than not, it could be a wild ride. Not in a sweet-mercy-I'm-going-down kind of way but in a hey-I-really-didn't-see-that-coming kind of way. When we throw our lot in with Jesus, he seems to upend all our careful planning and amazes us with how different his ways are from our own. And that is a good thing. When we realize our lives are not going the way we thought they would but we are aware we aren't in control and are holding on to God with all we've got, that is no small thing. It is an amazingly huge shift in the way we perceive God and how we are now coming to trust him, hope in him, and rely on him, even though we may not have a clue as to how our story is going to unfold.

The new perfect is realizing there is no perfect. There is no Eden on earth, but there is a path God will forge with us as we let him invade the dark corners of our lives and bring light and life to our souls. The new perfect is realizing that God takes our lives, the lovely and the broken, and molds them into a story that reflects him. It is focusing on the One who has saved us, and, even though we are a little scared and sweaty, waiting to see what he will do rather than trying to control or perfect our circumstances on our own. It is knowing that even though we have done some dumb things in the past, God can still hold our future and our freedom in the palm of his hand. I love what Paul says in Philippians: "No, dear friends, I am still not all I should be, but I am focusing all my energies on this one thing: Forgetting the past and looking forward to what lies ahead, I strain to reach the end of the race and receive the prize for which God, through Christ Jesus, is calling us up to heaven" (3:13–14).

You and I are in this race for real. We are forgetting the past and how we did things before and looking ahead to a new way of living, a way in which we let go, throw caution to the wind, and embrace all God has for us. We might be a little battered, a little winded, but we are in it totally and completely. And there is One person who is cheering us on, shouting encouragement, urging us to keep on doing what we are doing. Because what he wants more than anything is for us to succeed, to realize how much we need him, to know him for who he is, to soak up his grace and mercy. The Creator God sees you. He knows you. And he is thrilled with you, even if you are huffing and puffing (maybe that's just me). He's saying, "You can do it! I love you like crazy! Lean into me. Give me all your struggles, your mess-ups, your expectations, and your dreams, and I will come through for you." There is nothing to lose and everything to gain when we give up control, believe God is who he says he is, and run straight into his arms. It is the best finish to a race ever. So wherever you are, in whatever shape you are in, don't give up, press into him, and keep running. Because the good stuff is coming. (I love prizes, don't you?)

With that said, I pray this prayer for you found in Jude 1:24–25. Because Jude knew how to pray.

> And now, all glory to God, who is able to keep you from stumbling, and who will bring you into his glorious presence innocent of sin and with great joy. All glory to him, who alone is God our Savior, through Jesus Christ our Lord. Yes, glory, majesty, power, and authority belong to him, in the beginning, now, and forevermore. Amen.

Study Guide

Chapter 1: I Wish Eve Hadn't Eaten the Apple

1. Give three reasons you wish Eve hadn't eaten the apple.
2. What do you think it would have been like to talk to God face-to-face?
3. How do you experience "death in a thousand ways each day" in your own life?
4. If you could ask Eve one question, what would it be?

Chapter 2: I Would Listen to a Talking Snake

1. Do you recognize the voice of the snake in your own life? How?
2. What specific time did you listen to the lies of the snake rather than God's truth?
3. How do you reconnect with God when you feel yourself doubting or wavering in your trust of him?

Chapter 3: I Think God Is Holding Out on Me

1. In what area in your life do you feel or have felt like God is holding out on you?
2. If you took matters into your own hands, what was the end result?
3. What is something in your life that you desire right now that might not benefit you?
4. How does it change your perspective of God to know that he only wants to keep you from what can hurt you or destroy you?

Chapter 4: I Crave Apples and Other Things That Don't Satisfy Me

1. What do you crave more than anything right now?
2. What would it take for you to feel full?
3. How has God filled the needs in your life in the past?
4. What is the truth you need to believe about what you are craving right now?

Chapter 5: I Think I Need Some Fig Leaves to Cover Up My Shame

1. How do you relate to Adam and Eve recognizing their humanness?
2. What are some of the ways you try to cover up your mistakes?
3. Do you remember a time when you were scared about someone finding out you had messed up?

4. How do you feel knowing that when you admit your guilt, God can begin to flood your life with grace?

Chapter 6: I Want to Hide from God

1. Have you ever had a friend confront you on an area in your life? When?
2. When was the first time God called you out?
3. Is there anything you are hiding from God now? Why?
4. How do you respond knowing that God calls to you out of love?

Chapter 7: I Would Rather Not Take Responsibility for My Actions

1. When was the last time you had to own up to your sins?
2. Did you blame someone or something in your life or take the blame?
3. Have you found what Paul says, that you reap what you sow, to be true in your life? How?
4. When John says that God is faithful and just to forgive us our sins, does it change the way you view God? Why?

Chapter 8: I Have at Least One Enemy

1. Have you always been aware that you had an enemy in the snake?
2. On a scale of one to ten, how much power have you given him in your life?

3. How does your thinking shift when you realize that the battle against the snake has already been fought and won?

Chapter 9: I Feel Really Sad That There Is Pain in Childbirth

1. How do you deal with pain and brokenness in your life?
2. Do you try to escape your circumstances or control your circumstances?
3. In what areas of your life do you need healing right now?
4. Have you invited the One who formed you to heal those broken places in your life?

Chapter 10: I Have the Eden Gene

1. What is the life you dream of having?
2. How have you sensed the gap between the life you dream of and the life you are living?
3. Do you recognize the Eden gene in your own life? How?
4. Concerning what area in your life have you said to God, "I've got this"?

Chapter 11: I Am Exactly like Eve

1. Is there a specific situation in your life where you chose a path different from the one you knew God wanted you to choose?

2. How long was it before you realized that life without him was not all it is cracked up to be?
3. How does it revolutionize your life to know that no matter what you have done or how you have crossed him, he keeps coming after you with his love?

Chapter 12: I Am a Perfectionist

1. In what areas of your life do you strive to be perfect?
2. In what areas do you feel less than perfect?
3. Have you ever thought there is a chance you could be perfect?
4. How do you feel knowing that Jesus is the only One who is perfect and that he does not require it of you?

Chapter 13: I Get Discouraged

1. Do you find yourself getting discouraged in life? Why?
2. What are some unrealistic expectations you struggle with?
3. What or whom do you usually place your hope in?
4. How do the words of the psalmist David encourage you to change your expectations?

Chapter 14: I Have Control Issues . . . Big Ones

1. In what areas in your life do you fight for control?
2. Have you ever been so caught up in trying to control your life that your method of control began to control you? When?

3. How have you learned to trust God in areas of your life that you can't control?
4. Has there been a moment in your life when God made a path for you because you trusted him? What happened?

Chapter 15: I Don't Like Waiting

1. What are you waiting on in your life?
2. Has God promised you something that hasn't come to pass? What is it?
3. Do you find yourself discouraged, or do you trust that God is still at work in this area?
4. How do you gain strength from the Lord when you are waiting for him to answer your prayers and fulfill his promises to you?

Chapter 16: I Can Get a Little Bitter

1. Do you find yourself clinging to memories of the past? Is it because your past was great or terrible?
2. How does this affect how you see your future?
3. Do you relate to Naomi and her bent toward bitterness? Or toward Ruth's hopefulness?
4. How do you feel God is writing your story right now?

Chapter 17: I Am a Little Self-Centered

1. Do you find it difficult to take your focus off yourself? Why?

2. How do you relate to Jacob's family and their patterns of taking matters into their own hands?
3. How has Jesus changed you in your desire to follow him instead of centering your life around yourself?

Chapter 18: I Am a Rule Follower

1. Are you a rule follower or a rule breaker?
2. How does Jesus's dealings with the Pharisees cause you to examine your relationship with him?
3. Paul changed so radically when he came into contact with Jesus. Has Jesus's presence in your life shifted where your life was headed?

Chapter 19: I Am a Wreck

1. Has there ever been a time when you felt like a wreck? When?
2. How has the snake lied to you, causing you to have fear?
3. How does the way God showed Adam and Eve love, clothing them and caring for them, have a bearing on the wrecked places in your life?

Chapter 20: I Am in Denial

1. How do you feel the passage James 4:7–10 applies to you?
2. Are you in denial about your need for God in everyday life?

3. What are some of the ways God has lifted you up in your life?

Chapter 21: I Need a New Idea of What Perfect Looks Like

1. What is your normal way of viewing life?
2. How do you need Jesus to change you and your perception of the world around you?
3. Do you look at life like a Pharisee or like the blind man who knew he needed healing?
4. What would you do if Jesus stood before you and said, "I am the One who can heal you"?

Chapter 22: I Am Not in Control

1. Are you ready for God to begin to change you? How?
2. What is an area in your life that has already been changed by God?
3. When Paul talks about living by the Spirit, how is that different from how you are living?
4. How does it feel to admit you are not in control and to be willing to have the Holy Spirit direct you?

Chapter 23: I Need a Paradigm Shift

1. How does the knowledge that God loves you like he loves Jesus change the way you interact with him?
2. What are some of the ways you mirror your heavenly Father?

3. How do you want God to continue making a junior out of you?

Chapter 24: I Am Ready for a New Out-of-Control Me

1. What unbridled hope is motivating you past your fears?
2. How would you like God to transform your mind and your way of thinking?
3. How can you choose God daily in the parts of your life where you haven't chosen him before?
4. What do you think a life of freedom in Christ looks and feels like?

Sue would love to hear from you about your own Eve-ish experiences and your triumphs in your journey of following Christ.

- Connect with her via Facebook or email.
- Subscribe to her humorous newsletter, The Tired Supergirl Chronicles.
- Find out where she is speaking next or book her for your next women's event.

All this and more at www.susannaaughtmon.com.

To meet Sue and read about her take on life as a mom of three boys, a church planter's wife, and a writer, check out Sue's blog, *Confessions of a Tired Supergirl*, at tiredsupergirl.blogspot.com.

See you there!

Join the fun at **TiredSupergirl.com!**

Calling all supergirls!

- Join in a conversation with other tsgs (tired supergirls)
- Sign up for the *Tired Supergirl Chronicles* newsletter
- Check out the latest tired supergirl sightings

All this and more at **www.tiredsupergirl.com**

And check out Sue's blog,
Confessions of a Tired Supergirl,
at tiredsupergirl.blogspot.com
to meet Sue and read about her

- take on life as a mom of three boys, a church planter's wife, and a writer
- mishaps, cooking disasters, and other funny and familiar stories

See you there!

a division of Baker Publishing Group
www.RevellBooks.com

Available wherever books are sold.

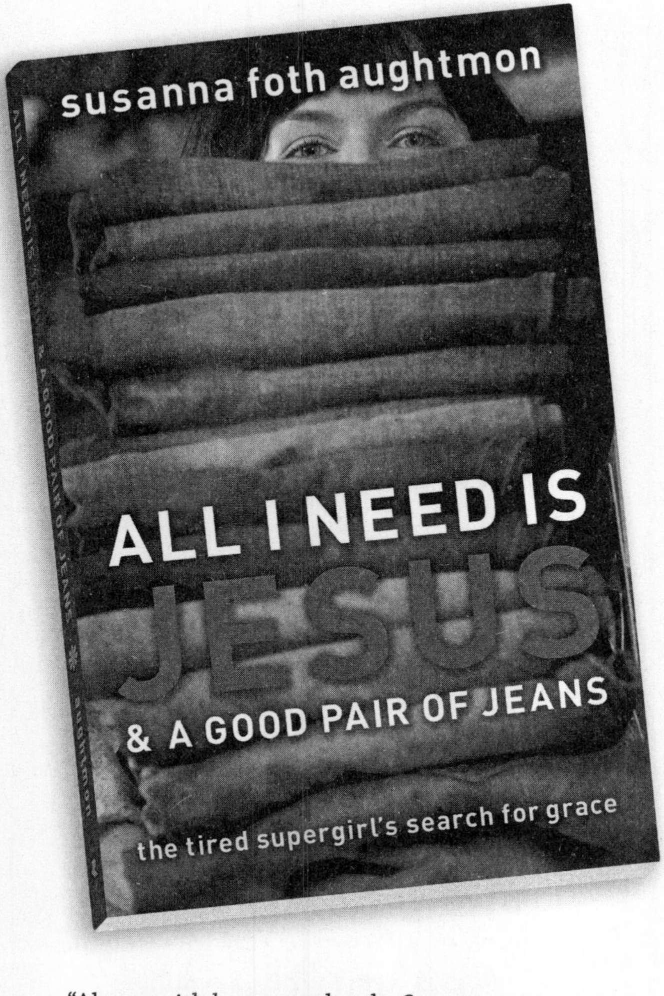